Gone Fishin'...
in N.J. Saltwater Rivers & Bays

Gone Fishin'...
in N.J. Saltwater Rivers & Bays

Manny Luftglass

Manny Luftglass T/A Gone Fishin' Enterprises
Box 556 • Annandale, NJ 08801

Pictured on the cover *(left to right)*: Four year young Jessica Gilbert with 1½ pound bluefish caught on mullet, 9/27/94, near the Route 72 Causeway.

Mike Pawlikowski, age 11, with blue claw crab measuring 6 inches from point-to-point, caught out of Oceanic Marina, 8/17/94.

Slightly older Ralph Knisell and 44 pound striped bass, caught in Delaware Bay, 11/13/94.

Pictured on the back: Author with 16 inch out-of-season fluke about to be released back into Great Bay.

*My first recollection of a fishing trip goes back to 1938
when my mother, father, brother and I fished at night for whiting
off of Steeplechase Pier in Coney Island.
We used two rods and shared them, catching lots of fish.
Both of my parents are now long gone
and never really acknowledged by me before in writing so,
to them,
Pauline, who died of cancer before she even reached age 41,
and to Harry, the guy who started me off
in this wonderful hobby/sport,
who also was killed by cancer at age 64,
my love and thanks.*

*Dad was a super fisherman
and Mom came along as often as she could.
He and I fished rivers and bays together hundreds of times.
One of the finest days that I can ever remember with him
was in a rowboat on the Manasquan River in the 70's,
with daughters Barbara and Sue helping us fill the bucket.*

*Again, this book is dedicated to the memories of
Harry and Pauline Luftglass,
may they continue to rest in peace,
but also sneak a look every now and then at the bald guy
with torn jeans in the back of his little toy boat
(formerly a kid with wild and long hair with torn jeans
in the back of someone else's little toy boat).*

Gone Fishin' In N.J. Saltwater Rivers & Bays
By Manny Luftglass

© 1995 Emanuel Luftglass

Published By
Manny Luftglass T/A Gone Fishin' Enterprises
Box 556 • Annandale, NJ 08801
Ninth Printing, 2004

ALL RIGHTS RESERVED.
No part of this book may be used or reproduced in any form or means
without the written permission of the author,
expect in cases of brief quotations.

ISBN 0-9650261-2-4
Publishers' Graphics, Carol Stream, IL 60188

Design & Typography:
TeleSet
Somerville, New Jersey

PRINTED IN THE UNITED STATES OF AMERICA.

Contents

Chapter 1: **The Attempt** 1

Chapter 2: **Location** 3

Chapter 3: **Laws And Enforcement** 4

Chapter 4: **Tackle Maintenance** 9

Chapter 5: **Tackle Itself** 12

      a: **Rods** 12

      b: **Reels** 13

      c: **Rigs 'n hooks** 13

      d: **Bait** 16

      e: **Sinkers** 18

      f: **Chumming** 19

      g: **Lures** 21

      h: **Other stuff** 22

Chapter 6: **Anchoring** 24

Chapter 7: **Raritan Bay** 26

Chapter 8: **Sandy Hook Bay** 36

Chapter 9: **Shrewsbury River** 42

Chapter 10: **Navesink River** 47

Chapter 11: **Shark River**	51
Map of Shark River	51
Chapter 12: **Manasquan River**	64
Chapter 13: **Toms River**	78
Chapter 14: **Forked River/Oyster Creek**	82
Chapter 15: **Waretown**	85
Chapter 16: **Long Beach Island**	88
Chapter 17: **Mullica River**	98
Chapter 18: **Great Bay**	102
Chapter 19: **Atlantic City Area**	107
Chapter 20: **Sea Isle City**	111
Chapter 21: **Avalon To Cape May**	114
Chapter 22: **Villas**	119
Chapter 23: **Maurice River**	122
Chapter 24: **Fortescue**	126
Seminar Notes	130
Personal Fishing Journal	132

Chapter 1

The Attempt

Since moving to New Jersey in 1964, I have fished all up and down its coastline, wandering from one area to another, usually motivated by what I read in fishing newspapers and columns, as well as by what others had told me.

We will talk about each month of the year, by location, telling you what kind of fishing to do, when, where, how, etc. In addition to that breakdown, *Gone Fishin' In Saltwater Rivers And Bays* will also give you other important details. I hope to be able to pin-point the boat rental facilities. Ditto the places where you can launch your small boat, ramps and otherwise. Folks who want to just park their car and sling lead will find shore locations in each chapter as well.

Let me apologize in advance if I screw up a spelling word or two. We have so many Indian-named locations alone along our coast that only a miracle could have kept me from messing up. If I had found a buck for every time I messed up the word Barnegat (or izzit Barnaget) alone, I could have paid the whole printing bill for this book.

I hope you will enjoy reading this book, and will learn more about the great fishing that we have here in New Jersey. While freshwater enthusiasts are a'plenty, and many people really do love to fish "out to sea," maybe the widest variety of fishing styles are practiced "inside," and clearly, this is where you want to bring the young people. For the most part, a young person can catch fish (or crabs) inside, not get seasick, and enjoy the one-on-one attention that can be obtained from the boat operator. There are few other ways to help a relationship prosper as much!

While this book will tell you a lot about the Garden State's inshore salt waters, for true, up-to-date information I suggest you consult *The Fisherman* magazine each week to get current reports. Certainly the writers who produce one or more columns every week for daily newspapers are prime sources of knowledge too, so make it your business to read Al Ristori in the *Star Ledger*, John Geiser in the *Asbury Park Press*, Mike Sheperd in the *Atlantic City Press*, Lou Rodia in the many South Jersey papers he writes for, and Russ Wilson's columns, wherever his by-lines appear. There are, of course, many other excellent writers to follow as well.

You will see little reference in this book to "headboats" or "charter boats," and that is because most of them fish out in the ocean. Many also fish "inside," so do not hesitate to try and arrange for a charter at a river or bay of your choice. Hop a "headboat" and try inside too. Many boats from Perth Amboy to Cape May, and then around up to Fortescue, fish rivers and bays as well as in the ocean.

CHAPTER 2

Location

We will drive down the coastline of New Jersey in this book, adding lots of coin to the Garden State Parkway authorities along the way. In fact I ran through a few packages of tokens during the effort. For those who like to go south to north, sorry, but the path driven and the story will head from Raritan Bay down to Cape May. We will even hang a right and travel up Delaware Bay a bit to Fortescue. I will omit most of the Delaware River above Fortescue because several other books exist that specifically talk about that fine river.

Again, for people with last names that start in the back half of the alphabet and hate being called last, and to you South Jerseyites who think a killy is a "minny," or a fluke is a "flounder," sorry, but it will be north to south.

CHAPTER 3

Laws And Enforcement

Perhaps the most important thing to learn about this is that no matter when I wrote this book, and when you bought it, laws do change. Do not take every word to be fact, because, again, laws are made to be changed. (No, NOT broken, changed.) Remember too that you will fish at times in bordering states where laws differ. Fluke and flounder lovers know that at times, New York and New Jersey had different size and bag limits and that made it tough to deal with. Striped bass enthusiasts too really need to have an up-to-date set of regs stapled to their arm. Ditto bluefish. Where caught for stripers and blues can determine how big a fish must be or how many you can take. Suffice it to say that most regulations make a lot of sense.

It just is not right to fish for stripers when they are dormant. Years back, guys would "fish" the Mullica for stripers when the fish were dormant. Their "lure" would be what salmon jerkers called "Tug flies" upstate New York. A huge, weighted treble hook, cast out and swung back wildly was the "lure." Funny, hardly any of these bass were caught in the mouth.

Another reg that makes sense is to leave spawning crabs go back unharmed. If you see eggs, drop 'em back in.

Flounder and fluke size limits make sense too but here people need to know how to keep a fish from bleeding and have to develop the ability to clip their leaders and release the fish with hook still inside. Properly released, most of these fish will survive the experience as salt water helps rust the hook away quickly.

Do we have overkill sometimes in law? Sure, and a few examples will follow.

Laws And Enforcement

My favorite fishing spot for fluke in the whole planet used to be in Sandy Hook Bay, alongside the right side of the pier at the Earle Ammunition Pier. The last buoy out was black first, and then green, numbered seven. In a ten year period I bet I caught no less than a thousand fluke within ten yards of the drop-off at this buoy. I was, however, breaking the law for a while. I do not go there any more. You see, Navy ships dock there, some near-permanently, and others, to load up with ammo.

As a young man I wore Navy blue part-time for eight years in the Naval "Ready" Reserve. One day we tied up at the exact spot I am talking about and I spilled some strange red stuff out of a big tin pitcher into cups held by other swabbies who were sweating their brains out. They were dragging five inch in circumference, fifty-five pound shells from dock to ship and had to stop for a drink every now and then. Fortunately for my skinny bones, I was a "mess cook" and did not have to do the muscle thing.

There was and still remains, a law that requires people to keep a substantial distance away from a military installation. One good reason is to avoid sabotage and another is for our own safety, while ammunition is being handled. Number one doesn't give a guarantee with a distance requirement because if some loony wanted to do harm, I doubt that a distance requirement would work.

Back in the 70's I had spoken to the executive officer of the pier, a Commander Bieber, as a fishing writer. After some discussion, he agreed with my feeling about number one, and we worked out a way to deal with number two. He agreed to allow fishing near the pier if and when no ships were at the dock AND being loaded.

The ground rules were that we could fish from the surrounding buoys OUT. Frankly, the best fishing was right on the edge of the channel anyway, at its extreme drop-off so fishing from the buoys out was perfect. Most of that fishing I did was therefore legal. People were notified of this change in my fishing columns and elsewhere, but one day, Commander Bieber was transferred! From then on, it was hell!

I fished near that buoy one day on anchor, in my eight foot "Karp Katcher," and had a mess of fluke when a marine police boat came charging up and whacked me in the bow. Thus clanked, it could only follow that THEY would yell at ME, and indeed they did, saying that I was violating the law. I suppose they thought the entire bow of my yacht was lined with atomic bombs and I was chased, first being warned about the magnitude of the fine that I could have gotten.

Warnings were shouted at fishermen from the pier itself via bullhorns, telling us what kind of trouble we would be in but one day, the Marine Police and Coast Guard guys that had been chasing us were joined by a zillion foot long Navy tug. This crew really had a ball enforcing the law. Instead of yelling, the tug just went past the fishing boats, stopped, and started to back up. Did you ever see a gadillion pound tug boat charging backwards at flank speed? Man, you really could see a tidal wave that way, or so it seemed. This did get our attention. Enough yelling and hollering, topped by this thing, and I have not been back in ten years or so.

I do not want to down play the importance of safety for all, but really, Uncle Navy, give us a break. I spoke to a well known legislator about this a few years back and his reply was, instead of an offer to help, "You do not live in my district." Good huh? How about the thousands of fishermen who do live there who cannot enjoy the location? His secretary even told me that one day, she and her husband were chased also.

Another incident took place in Sandy Hook involving a friend of mine who shall remain nameless. He was in his 70's at the time and had launched his little boat off of the beach behind his home. It was summer, and his attire consisted of a pair of shorts, period, with pockets empty. After catching a few fluke, a boat approached and the guy in uniform asked to see his boat operating license. My friend told the uniform that it was home in his wallet and he wound up getting a ticket! Nice, huh? Instead of letting him go and get the wallet, slam, fine!

One of the silliest examples took place in my third yacht, an 11 foot ten inch long Grumann rowboat, anchored in the Shark River Inlet, east of the Route 71 Bridge. A different senior citizen than the guy we just spoke about was in the bow of the "Gone Fishin'" and we were catching some nice winter flounder. It was early in June and it was the first year that a size limit went into effect on fluke.

We fished for fluke with one rod and flounder with another, and had several dozen flounder already in the bucket as I swung another into the boat. Three undersized fluke had also been caught and released. A uniformed officer saw me swing the flounder a'board and had his companion approach us. The tide was moving out and in this place, it really can crank. The bow seat was well filled by my buddies large bottom and we had three buckets, and other assorted stuff in the tin boat. The officer held onto the starboard side of my boat and asked how many fluke we had caught. I told him "three," and he figured he had seen one and could now write us up for three undersized fish. I told him though that we had thrown them all back. He tried to board my yacht and nearly turned it over, since he was big and the boat was small, leaving no room for even both of his feet. It would have been a funny sight, I guess, if the boats separated and he did a magical split but no such luck would take place. I finally handed him the bucket and he was very upset to find that all the fish were flounder. Miffed, off he went.

Do we have laws that exist and are properly written? You bet. My thanks to Dave Chanda of The Department of Fish, Game & Wildlife for sending me the regulations that were current at the end of '94, but again, they do change.

If you want to get a copy of the latest, up-to-date rules, write to The Office of Information and Education, CN400, Trenton, N.J. 08625-0400, and I am sure they will send you what you want. Remember, please, proper regs need to be complied with — be it crab size, clamming rules, open or closed seasons, etc.

Do we need to have a saltwater fishing license on the other hand? My vote is, as loud as I can make it, HELL NO!

You do need to know who can operate a boat, what type of license is needed to do so, and so on. What speed you can run at, where you can anchor, rules regarding alcohol, all must be known.

I remember that a friend told me that some years back, Coast Guard records revealed that of male bodies recovered in South Jersey waters, most had their flies open! Were these people drinking? We know what else they were doing. Avoid booze while on the water, and bring a "potty" too, please.

🐟 NOTE 🐟

In this 1997 reprint I must tell you that there were significant changes in the law in just two years since I first wrote this book! For example, law was changed to make the taking of winter flounder illegal during January and February so while I tell you throughout the book how to catch flounder during these months, unless law is changed again, sorry—don't do it, or at least throw them back. Personally, I would like to see a modest bag limit during those two months only to allow those few that do go fishing then to keep a couple of fish for a meal. These are spawning months so the basic idea is pretty good, but maybe this law is too harsh. Laws change, as warned, so check them out before you accidentally violate one.

FLASH   *FLASH*

So now we have our Ninth Edition, printed in January of 2004, and we have to warn you again that lots more new rules have been passed. Besides Closed Seasons on both flatfish, we also have regulations regarding many other fish so be warned that you really must know the law or be ready to be fined, okay? The bottom line is that if you are uncertain, practice "Catch and Release"!

Chapter 4

Tackle Maintenance

My expertise surrounding mechanical devices consists of knowing that the yellow end of the screw driver is the one that you are supposed to hold onto. For tackle maintenance, I try to just keep using the stuff, but to wash it all off often. This is the best medicine. The following section was written for us by Don Madson, owner of Sportsmen's Outfitter in Clark, N.J. He really knows tackle maintenance, and he volunteered to help with these details. I have taken the liberty of cutting and hacking some stuff out and revising other words, but for the most part, these thoughts are his, not mine.

Don looks at this subject as something to do after you are done fishing for "the season," to help keep your sanity intact as well as a way to avoid the repair bill.

Let's start with one rod, and if no one else is at home (if so, a call to the asylum will surely be placed before too long) repeat the process with all the others too. Take it into the shower with you, maybe lining the others up nearby. Share the soap first with your best expensive-to-replace graphite wonder. Sluicing the thing down with soapy water removes salty sludge pretty well. Take a toothbrush to the feet of the guides and the reel seat. Cheap maintenance, especially if you can snag a free sample or two from your dentist. (I do not recommend using HER toothbrush.)

The reels aren't much more difficult. In order to give basic attention to them, either conventional or spinning, use a basic rule of thumb. If you can reach it, clean it. If it moves, grease it. Not too much grease and maybe by this time, you should also be out of the shower.

It's often a bad idea to open up a reel and attempt to service it, especially if you haven't done it before. Don regularly takes care of reels that are brought into his shop in a bag, in many pieces, often with one or two missing.

Be satisfied with taking care of the outside if the innards scare you. Soap and water works pretty well with reels too, but be sure to rinse them well and be cautious about getting water inside the gear case (many of the gears are made of steel or pot metal). WD-40 and CRC are good water displacing protectors, but use of them alone does not take the place of proper cleaning and some lines may not react well chemically with the spray stuff so be careful.

Conventional reels do not require much more treatment than spinning models, except that relatively close attention should be given to anything that costs more. If you are comfortable cleaning up the expensive lever drags, fine, otherwise Don can do it for you. Ditto lots of other quality stores up and down our state. By the way, it's a good idea to push the drag lever forward when you wash down the conventional reels to keep water out of the drag system.

Cotton swabs are indispensable tools for reel cleaning. If you are not comfortable using the brush-and-solvent method of cleaning them, just spray the innards with some WD-40 and clean up with the swabs. The same goes for the components, gears, oscillation blocks, etc., that you will find inside the body of the reels. (Right, Don, remember I only know that you hold the yellow end of the screw driver, and that when I pull the rope in back of my boat and a noise comes out of the machine, I know I can go fishing.)

Drag disks, with a few exceptions, should have a slight amount of lubrication. Many of us older guys will remember when all drag washers were made of leather, interspersed with brass disks. The leather washers were soaked in the favorite lubricant of the day (Vaseline, motor oil, cup grease, etc.), and put to work. Today's drag systems are made of Teflon and other synthetic fibers, graphite, titanium, stainless steel, nickeled brass, and other "Ghee Whiz" combinations. The day's of the thumb pad brake system on reels are all over.

Madson prefers a light, even application of grease such as "blue grease" on all drag disks except Teflon. He said that Penn does not believe that their HT-100 disks should be greased, and that the glaze that forms in the fiber disks doesn't diminish the efficiency of the drag. Too much grease will cause slippage and too little will cause the washers to bond together into a stack of disks and washers that will do little to slow down a fish. In any case, if you keep the system clean, problems with your drag will be minimized.

Chapter 5

Tackle Itself

a: Rods

Most people take two or three rods into the boat with them each day and I am not much different. Besides needing at least one spare in case a monster hauls one overboard, or breaks a rod, etc., there are other reasons too. Obviously the size of the fish you are after will be a significant reason to use different weight rods but there is another key reason to go with different rod size.

On a good, moving tide, no matter what part of the state you are fishing, it is nearly impossible to come anywhere near bottom on an ultra-lite type stick. Please forgive me if this is too basic for you, but you would never guess how many guys go flounder fishing in fast moving water with only a light freshwater rod. Did you ever see what a three ounce sinker can do to a light wand? 'Tis not a pretty sight. This is a sight, however, often seen on headboats and these fellows will make you crazy all day long as they hang up with people, no matter what skill they may have.

Take the light rod for flounder, fluke, weakies, porgies, and even for such as slammer blues and stripers, if you are alone in your own boat, but still have a far heavier and stiffer rod too. It is an absolute must that this stick be in the boat so that you have a chance at staying near bottom with the needed heavier weight. I personally like the long "flippin' stick" that I use because it is graphite, super sensitive, and can handle darn near anything. I have even used it in the ocean, drifting for whiting with a five or six ounce sinker.

An ultra-lite type, plus a medium weight spinning rod for most fishing, and my stiff bait caster always are on board the "Gone

Fishin' " while fishing rivers and bays.

Surf rods are often helpful in slinging lead, especially from Raritan Bay beaches for stripers, but please leave them at home if you are after smaller fish. The dummy on the headboat with a pole that can poke your eye out with ease is not my friend. They really look silly too, with one end of the rod nearly touching the other in a cooking tide.

b: Reels

Here again, go with several and make sure that you wash each completely quickly after use. Salt water will certainly weaken your line if not washed but more importantly can destroy the innards of a reel. No matter how tired you are, wash it off.

Match the rod, certainly, so if using a small reel, use an ultra-lite rod too and only six or eight pound mono. On the medium weight stick I like a similar spinning reel with ten pound line. The stiff rod usually has 12 to 15 pound mono. I do not use the new-fangled lines that have nearly no stretch because my pea-brain has not learned yet how to tie a knot in the stuff that will hold well. I have used it and have had wonderful luck in breaking it on a set so, maybe later.

Leave the surf sticks home unless you are slinging from shore, but if that is your style, by all means, do it. Mount larger spinning reels on the rod instead of conventional, because the revolving spool backlash that we all experience from time to time could cause severe injury to the guy near you as he falls down in a heap, laughing like a hyena.

c: Rigs n' Hooks

From time to time, I certainly use "rigs," but by and large, the best rig for me is no rig at all. That little plastic baggie that comes all set up with three-way, barrels, tubes, whistles and tweaters, plus hooks are not for me. There are a few occasions when I go with the more modest varieties but generally, I tie my own leadered hooks on conventional mono.

Exceptions occur in moving tide. A fluke "rig," with stiff three foot leader often works well. Ditto the winter flounder pre-tied deal that has fifteen pound or so stiff leader, with two properly spaced number eight silver carlisle hooks, above which containing a yellow or red plastic bead. Some like this rig prepared with a gold english bend hook too in size eight or so. For my early fall fishing, going after porgies, seabass, etc., I will generally go with size six eagle claw type hooks with bait holder, tied into stiff fifteen pound mono. This is because of tide, usually. You see, fast tide movement requires stiffer mono and stronger hooks.

The pros who fish stripers, weakfish, etc., with bait, generally do use a swivel, three way or barrel, to let the bait work better, but simple is better sometimes here too.

Back in the 70's I remember Captain Charlie Selby of the Wildwood-based party boat, "Rainbow," telling me that he did not like rigs either when fishing Delaware Bay for fluke (they call them "flounder" down thattaway), but he insisted on cutting off any hook that had any rust at all on it every trip. The hook simply had to be gold in color, he added, and usually an english bend in size two-oh or so.

Another skipper who went simple was Captain Billy Van who took his "Captain Bill" out of Belmar for fluke, going with nothing but the most plain set up. If that was the way to go in the ocean, I feel that inside water requires that style even moreso.

If any of you have read either of my "reservoir" books you will know that I virtually NEVER use any other hook in Round Valley or Spruce Run than a 3906 Mustad Sproat in size six. Well, here again, being a creature of habit, my winter flounder fishing on slow moving tide from a boat involves one kind of hook only, with two varieties.

Certain to create controversy, the hook is a number ten Mustad in Viking model. Some freshwater folks use this for tying wet flies but for me, it presents a piece of worm or clam to the fish the very best way possible, naturally. Most of the time I use the longer shank model, an inch or so, but in the coldest of water I go with the short shank, again, to present a bait that is easiest to eat and most attractive too. I tie this hook on a fifteen inch strip of limp ten

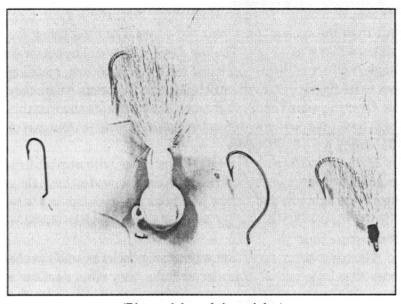

(Pictured from left to right.)
#10 Mustad Viking — weighted White Bucktail, size 1-0 —
Gold English Bend, size 4 — and #2 Non-weighted White Bucktail.

pound mono, going with two hooks, tied together in the standard manner. After having caught thousands of flounder on this style hook, IN SLOW WATER, please believe me that it is best.

When the tide is moving I go with the more standard number eight or ten carlisle on stiffer mono, and find no personal difference between use of beads or not, although many guys swear by them.

Here's one for the shore caster only. Instead of fishing for flounder from a bulkhead or pier with the typical two hooks falling below the sinker rig, just tie on one hook. You will see a huge difference in the numbers of times your leaders will tangle into the line above the sinker this way. Again, light mono and skinny wire hook in little or no tide movement, but stiffer on both if the tide is moving faster. O-k, we went with a hook falling below, but now tie another leadered hook in, well ABOVE the sinker. Yes, flounder are only on bottom so why a higher hook? The leader should only be six inches or so. Tie it in a foot or so above the sinker and yes, on its face, that makes no sense at all, right? Well, think it out. Cast out from the dock and set your rod down. The hook below the sinker will rest at bottom. The one above, with your line out on an angle, will actually dust back and forth across bottom, reaching out to feeding flounder, and still being right at bottom where they lie. Over the years I have caught more flounder from shore on this high hook than on the one below the sinker, no matter what part of the state I have fished from.

Fluke hooks? Again, different than most, I go with number four english, tied onto twenty pound limp mono cut two feet long. Here again, the light line and skinny wire hook present a bait in a very life-like manner and in smaller bodies of water, I find the fish to be much more finicky.

The big problem some find when using hooks as small as the ones that I use is that, flounder or fluke, they often swallow a hook. While this takes place more often than it does with the bigger, stiffer hooks that most use, I am also catching many more fish than they are. The difference is that, as with my reservoir hook, I keep plenty of spares on board and if I cannot see the hook as I examine a fish that is to be released, the line is clipped and away the fish goes, not too much harmed. The hook will rust out shortly and most fish will survive. The key is to either take the fish out of the water gently without causing it to bleed, or even better, reach over and cut the leader with the fish in the water. Yes, this could cost you a nickel or a dime hook each time, but big deal!

Folks slinging bait for stripers or blues cannot get away with light hooks so here, go more conventional. Walleye Walleye, who we will shortly hear from, likes to tangle with big blues with ultra lite stuff, but a sizable hook and a light wire leader too.

d: Bait

Captain Marty Haines calls it "filleting," but by any other name, something that too few people do often works best for winter flounder, and it is even the cheapest thing also! Not easy to get anymore, a fresh sea clam, called "skimmer," makes dynamite bait. I like them for flounder, stripers, porgies, blowfish, etc., but if fresh ones are not available, most stores carry ones that are frozen, whole out of the shell, in a bag of three or four. This is a good substitute. When on a crowded party boat, look at the guy with the dopiest outfit. He is also the fellow who uses that stringy muscle that is around the inner edges of the clam. He will often fish for an hour without losing bait, but also without catching fish. This is usually too stiff and the flatties do not like it. If you want to bust on him though, tell him that it is "REALLY GOOD." The clam "tongue," that large orange mass in the center, is what Marty and I "fillet." Place it flat on a board and simply cut it into two halves, through the center. Sam Krugler of the Woodstream Rod & Gun Club taught me to then use the blunt end of my knife to "tenderize it," tapping one half equally and then cutting it into strips of a quarter inch wide by an inch and a half long. This piece of bait will wiggle and actually chum for you as it oozes the stuff you loosened with the knife. The brownish membrane that clings to the inner part of the shell can be gently removed and, wound around on your hook. This is even better bait in cold water for nuts like me who work hard for our fish.

Skimmer clams make great bait for lots of fish, not just flounder, and never go out without some, regardless of what kind of fish you are after.

Sedge mussels? Honestly, I do not know where you can obtain any of these gray, ribbed members of the bivalve family legally, but if and when you do, they are the best bait you can find for flounder.

Sand and bloodworm are standard baits and different sections of the state find one preferred greatly to the other. From Barnegat south, hardly anyone will use a sandworm, for example, so let's simply say that most worm users below that area go with bleeders only. My guess is that fellows fishing weakfish inside in Cape May County use whole sandworms but do not tell anyone about it, and I do recommend bringing some south too. Some people swear that there is no difference in leaving the head on or cutting it off, but I personally feel that the only place that a sandworm head belongs is off your hook. I always cut it off, period. On the other hand, the head of a bloodworm, dangled below the hook barb, somehow will cause even more bites so try that. The softer and older the worm, especially the bleeders, the better the coldest water winter flounder prefer it, believe it or not.

Tapeworms are not just things you get from eating bad food. Striper and flounder nuts dig their own and swear that they are the best bait going. You can find some a few feet long, so I do not suggest asking a squeamish member of your party to cut one into pieces of bait for you. They gush ooze, and while that is good for fish, it is bad for weak tummies.

Fresh bunker or herring are top baits going for striped bass and some bluefish too, but not easy to get. Many of the tackle stores we will talk about here carry both in season though. Herring cut into strips are wonderful for fluke. Down south a bit into the state, chunks of them are gobbled by bluefish and fluke alike.

If you can get them, fresh peanut mullet are spectacular bait, for anything from blues to stripers, and weakfish to big fluke.

Grass shrimp, live first, and even frozen, produce superb fishing for weakfish and kingfish, and do not disregard supermarket shrimp either, going with the cheaper medium sized critters.

I saw a guy fishing the Manasquan Inlet in February and he was using a hunk of bacon! Oh yeah, he had not caught anything either. He did say that one day in November he caught several sundial fluke on it though.

Live spot or small snapper are hardly ever used, but the pro's who do catch some of the biggest fluke around. A strip of fresh caught spot produced a bunch of weakfish for me one day at Fortescue.

A live eel, kept cold so that you have a chance of putting it on the hook before it strangles your arm, is favored by the striper guys, as many of you already know.

e: Sinkers

Personal preference generally is involved here, but some just do not work. Eliminate the use of pyramid sinkers in nearly all inside water, please. The surf pole with pyramid deal on a flounder boat, winter or summer flounder, often is being held by a poor soul who everyone is laughing at behind his back. Striper fishing from Raritan Bay can work this way, but with the sinker rigged to allow the leadered hook to slide up and down instead of being tight to the line.

Egg sinkers have become a great choice, especially for folks after weakfish. The smaller the better. I love to use one, stopped by a barrel swivel, below which I add a two foot leadered fluke hook. Anchored and casting across tide, as the sinker rolls and slides, many a fluke will take hold. This set-up will also allow a fluke to run a bit, ditto weakfish, before you set and until then, he never knew someone was upstairs waiting to hurt him. I bet I caught several hundred fluke in Sandy Hook Bay while casting an egg sinker and bringing the killy and squid strip back. Typically, your hit will be harder from fluke this way, but often it is just a stop, extra weight, and then you slam it home.

Standard bank sinkers are most popular and here the manner is to use enough to hold bottom.

Folks like flat or rounded sinkers with metal attachment on top and this is a favorite method with me.

The "Dipsey" sinker, a variety of the above, but teardropped in shape, allows you to fish in a variety of ways. I remember Captain Pete Del Rossi, of the charter boat, "L'il Mia," teaching me how to keep my reel in free spool in Fortescue as I allowed this small sinker to roll out in the tide and drag my bait down with it. Weakfish and fluke respond very well to this slightly moving but controlled drift style.

f: Chumming

There are a few methods of chumming that work well while fishing inside, and most common is the style for winter flounder. Simply, by one manner or another, flounder respond to the appearance of food in their smelling area, and that area is virtually always, DOWNTIDE. The first rule that cannot be bent is that your chum must approach the fish from uptide, and your baited hooks must be in that path.

Whether swinging on a single anchor, or with two anchors in bottom, the chum needs to be placed uptide. The lighter the chum, and the stronger the tide, the higher above your hooks the chum must first appear. The easiest way is to use a chum pot with frozen chum log placed inside. Broken up clams and mussels, the black ones that cling to piers or those grayish ones talked about earlier, possibly illegal to gather, are great inside a pot. You may need to put a few heavy sinkers in the pot first if the tide is strong.

You really want to go either of two ways with a pot. Let a few feet of slack out after hitting bottom, OR tighten the chum pot line as it just hits bottom. If you let slack, you will need to jerk it up and down from time to time to release bait. On a tight line, with any kind of up and down boat movement at all, this will move chum out all by itself. Do remember to adjust your chum pot line every now and then to allow for rising or falling tides.

Take a friend with you on a headboat and fish exactly the same way, same bait, rigs, etc., but place him above the pot and you downstream of the pot. Tell him you did this for his own benefit. You may double his catch but let him know that it was your skill, not the chum that attracted fish firstly to your hooks.

I like to tie my pot into the point of the bow if single anchored, with no slack. This lets the boat chum for me as it bounces up and down in passing wakes.

Folks like to use a mess of clam or mussel, broken vigorously up into one of those red onion sacks, with sinkers inside. Sometimes this works better than a pot. Others simply will break up whole skimmer clams, if fresh, and drop them overboard. I really like this method and in slow tides, drop the clams at the downtide edge of the boat. In moving water, place them on the uptide side.

Breaking and stomping on mussels will really help, making sure to drop them over up tide to let them fall in a path that will bring fish to you.

Grass shrimp, fed slowly into the tide, will bring weakfish right close to your boat and whether it be the Manasquan, Barnegat, or the Mouth of the Mullica, this style works. One day I fished a charter boat named the "Frieda," a craft as old as the name implies, out of the Forked River area, and the skipper chummed from the port quarter and also fished. Needless to say, he caught more weakies than any of us, because his baited hooks were placed closest to the fishes path.

This reminds me a trip in May a few years back with Don Kamienski in which he chummed and fished a similar part of his own boat while we were on anchor in Great Bay. He was chumming with chunks of fresh herring that he had caught in the Delaware and we were after bluefish. By dumb luck, I managed to match his catch of three blues even though he had "the angle." We each also caught and released a bunch of out of season fluke, to 3 or 4 pounds.

Some great fluke catches are made while on anchor on channel edges via the chumming method. Clam or mussel in your pot works, but here some prefer a frozen ground bunker log.

The frozen bunker log releases chum evenly into the tide and it can produce snapper blues and porgies, along with other fish.

Do not disregard chumming while fishing a river or bay, it nearly always will help. Do not overchum though, and sometimes a fast tide will bring the fish way downstream of where you are fishing. In fact, chum less in a fast tide, and make sure the chum falls well above your hooks. Try to bring a heavy sashweight with you, tied on a heavy line. Banging this up and down on bottom, uptide, is good for many varieties of fish.

A peculiar method of "chumming" is produced by placing the smell right on your baited hook. Gene Zafian told me once that he proved clearly to himself that action was greatly improved by actually spraying some WD-40 right on his hook! By now you probably know too that spray smells, be it bunker oil or something like that, can dramatically add to your catch too. A form of "Dr. Juice" could not hurt.

g: Lures

We will talk throughout this book about a variety of methods that are used to catch striped bass inside most of our waters.

Frankly, the styles and lures change from place to place, as well as from season to season. I highly recommend you contact our local tackle stores that we talk about here for their own opinions. Honestly, they are the ones to ask.

Stripers to the side, bluefish enthusiasts really go with a variety of silver stuff. It could be a Kastmaster, ava-type jig, maybe Hopkins, if it does not shine and flutter, change over. As to the ava-style, some really like a "clean" jig, one with no tube at all. Others like fluorescent tubes. My own manner of fishing usually involves a clean jig that I add a six or seven inch black grape jelly worm onto. I buy them by the bag because you nearly always have to change worms after every bluefish bite, but the wiggle of these worms, in my opinion, substantially adds to your hit total.

Jigs of varied kinds are also talked about in chapters that follow, but make sure you have several with you because the real pro's swear by jigs for fluke and weakfish.

A form of lure that I started to use about fifteen years ago is silly simple, but it also does really work. A plain white bucktail HOOK, not a weighted jig, is what I really like for fluke! The hook should be small, only a size two or so, with red thread wrapping. I put a six inch stiff mono snell on it and tie it ten inches or so above my sinker while fluking. Adding a piece of bait, usually a smaller killy to the hook, you cannot imagine how many fluke lift just up off bottom to go after this. The biggest fluke of the day will get hooked this way often. I caught a six pounder near Leonardo on such a hook and a monster weakfish another time.

h: Other Stuff

Nets! Make sure you leave the little trout net at home and bring one with a big, wide mouth, and a handle that is pretty long too. When the tide is moving you may find it nearly impossible to reach a big fish, holding in the tide, two feet out further than your net handle can reach. This can make you hope to be much, much taller. Test the net mouth before leaving the house too. They can rot and a big fish escaping through the newly caused hole will equally get you sad.

Booze. Please, please, please, leave it all at home. Beer or hardstuff, forget it if you can because alcohol and water do not mix. Remember the story above about dead guys in the water with their flies open? I believe it to be dead true.

Kids. The very best thing to bring with you for a short trip on a tolerably warm day! Hardly ever, two kids, because two are a zillion times more than one. No, I do not count funny either. If you are after winter flounder, do it for a half-day, not a whole one. In your own boat for porgies and snapper, again, a few hours, plus lots of cookies and soda. Prepare for frequent bathroom needs too. When taking a young person with you, try to do as little fishing as possible so that the kid will really get your personal, undivided attention and help. This can really bring you so very close together, trust me.

Food. Sure, but in a cooler, and more than you think you will need, because a good day on the water will make you hungry enough to eat a bear.

Cooler. This itself is critical. A good mess of fish will turn into just that, A MESS, unless you keep them fresh, on ice. Not in a bucket of warming water, in a cooler with ice, and preferably one with an open drain to let the melted water out. Try putting a stringer of fish over for three or four hours in heat, and your stringer will contain garbage as the warm water destroys your catch.

CHAPTER 6

Anchoring

First, let's make sure you are in a big enough boat to safely anchor. Forget the canoes or "John-boats." Neither is meant for open salt water. Be certain that your boat has a high bow, not one that is low to the water. Anchoring such a boat in moving water with passing boats could drag the bow into the water and bring much of the river on board.

Match the anchor weight to the size of the boat. If in doubt, ask a facility that specializes in boating materials. My 14 foot 5 inch high bow bench seat Sea Nymph works well with a four pound Danforth style anchor AT BOTH ENDS OF THE BOAT. I have a five or six foot chain tied into the anchor line which hooks into the anchor. Some like claws and others, Navy style, with still more using mushroom anchors. For me, it is a Danforth with chain, matched to the boat.

When a tide is moving it is often difficult and sometimes unsafe to anchor with two so if in doubt, go with one anchor only. Make sure you have "ANCHOR LINE," not clothes line or that nasty, yellow curly cue stuff that creates knots that are impossible to untangle.

If you are in an area that many boats travel past, and are using two anchors, make sure the bow is facing the channel and boat traffic. A big wave that hits the bow is not fun. If set up with stern facing waves, this is less than fun, it is dangerous as the waves break over the opening for the motor.

Set on an angle sometimes helps, with one anchor less than half-way up tide. This places the boat in a quarterly angle to the tide and the end that faces downtide will beat up, fish count wise,

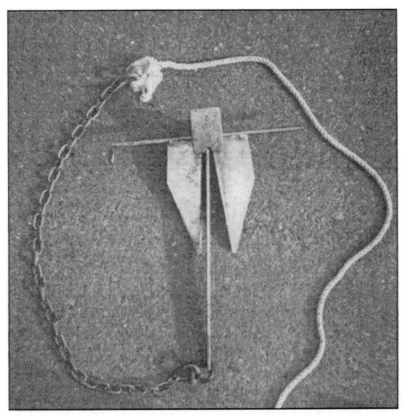

Danforth Anchor with chain. Note the expert Navy Knot.

on the other end.

It is particularly important to either be the owner of the boat or have a stupid friend to take you out when fishing on anchor. As many as 90% of the fish caught will be taken from the stern of the boat. Let the other guy have the bow where all the extra room is. Man, what a nice person you are. Stand crowded with buckets all around you as he sits in comfort. As the tide just starts to turn, change places with him though, because the front of the boat will do better on the first half-hour of the turn.

Chapter 7

Raritan Bay

This very large body of water is under fished to the extreme. Just look on a New Jersey map and you will see how large it is. Raritan Bay lies in two states, New York and New Jersey and that can make for substantial confusion regarding rules and regulations. For example, New York had a 14 inch size limit for fluke when we here in Jersey had a 13 inch limit. Now that the two states have the same size rule, it is a little bit easier.

Raritan Bay holds superb striped bass fishing, along with bluefish. Flounder and fluke call it home and I remember that a sturgeon was even hooked in the bay a few years back. When thinking about fishing in the Garden State, do not exclude this very productive body of water.

We have party and charter boats that frequent Raritan Bay, along with lots of boat ramps, a rental dock or two, and for inshore fishing, this body of water offers more action for guys fishing from land than anywhere else in the state! Read on and we will discover the bay together. Honestly, I am as guilty as most, having spent less time here, closer to my home than anywhere else. To get details to share with you about the bay, I interviewed several experts and here is what I was able to find out.

Picking parts of the year apart from each other, we start with the first and coldest threesome, a time that most people agree it is far better to spend in Florida. I did spend part of that time in 1995 in that state, but most of the rest of January through March was devoted to obtaining these details, trying to figure out what my scribbled notes meant, and then poking it into the computer. Here goes.

In the event of a late winter, like '95, flounder can still be taken on warm days in January in the bay, and when the winter is very mild, an early appearance of flounder will occur late in March. There used to be an early fishery at Cliffwood Beach but once sand was added by government to help with erosion, this messed that up. Staten Island, between Princess Island and Perth Amboy has some early life. So does Union Beach but truthfully, the experts agree that reading, T.V., Fishing Shows, and even WORK are better things to do at that time of the year.

April through June are among the best months of the year in the bay. I talked to Pat Scaglione, owner of Scag's B&T in Staten Island and he told me a little about the fishing on his side of Raritan Bay. Pat's store is on the north side of the island, and since that is strictly New York and this is a "Joisey" book, we spoke about the south side, facing our state. He feels that Princess Bay is where to start flounder fishing in the spring on incoming tide. Seguine Point near Lemon Creek at the Princess Bay Boatman's Association on high tide is a good spot. The Conference House towards Highland Boulevard is another flattie place.

Princess Harbor is good for trolling schoolie bass. A favorite place for Pat is off of Highland Boulevard behind Carmen's Restaurant where you can walk to a stone barge and plug first bass, then blues and later some weakfish. The bogs at Great Kills Park is another place to throw swimming plugs as well as bucktails with Mr. Twister tails. Watch your step here, the bottom is filled with deep holes!

Next to help out was Captain Marty Haines of the Perth Amboy based party boat, "Sea Pigeon IV." Marty is well known for bottom fishing and of course with his boat, most of the fishing is done out in the ocean. That does not mean that he never fishes the bay. On the contrary, both flatfish have come over his rails in goodly numbers. I remember catching a mess of them one day on the Sea Pigeon only a few minutes from his dock! 1994 was an unusual year in Marty's area, with the ocean usually being too cold for good fluke fishing, so he spent a lot of time in the bay that year. Again though, most years, he fishes outside.

Captain Haines generally starts fishing each year in the 3rd to last week in March in Raritan Bay, often on the Staten Island side off of Great Kills. This area is fine after a mild winter, but if bitter, like '94 was, April is a better jumping off time. Please do remember that New York came out with new regulations regarding flounder fishing in their waters and Staten Island is indeed a part of that State! As of 1/1/95 no fisherman could keep a flattie until 3/17! Top that off with a 15 flounder possession limit and an 11 inch size requirement and you may need a Maritime lawyer to help out with all the rules. That means that, even if it was a mild winter, forget the New York side until it is legal to fish. In our laws and enforcement chapter we spoke about this in greater length but suffice it to say that the magical line which separates our water from New York's water can be drawn in strange ways.

Marty likes Great Kills in April and into mid spring when he runs a bit farther over to some areas in the middle of the bay around Keyport. Some old clam beds exist here. As with all flounder fishing, you do need to chum and he does plenty of it.

Fluke action starts yearly in the middle of May but again, make sure you are into "Open season," as called for by the law. The Sea Pigeon fishes the Bug Light, plus Hoffman and Swinburne Islands early, and then as the fluke enter the bay deeper, often finds good action at the Great Bed Light House near the Western end of the Raritan Reach. I really banged them one day here some years back with Marty. He fishes this spot early in the day often, especially when tide and wind are running together from the beach out. A good drift can take you clear out three quarters of the way into the bay with fluke all along the trail. Just remember, fish shallow early in the season and then as the water warms up, make your drifts deeper.

1994 was, as I said earlier, unusual with much of the action inside, but normally, Marty takes the big boat out to sea and we will talk about the ocean in another book to follow.

Come early fall yearly, the Sea Pigeon is often found in the bay again, with folks ringing the rail and filling their pails with lots of porgies and seabass, as well as blackfish. The snags and rocks around West Bank are a favorite location and fiddler crabs produce blackfish while the people baiting with worms, usually bloodworm, beat up on large sand porgies. Skimmer clam can catch all of these fish, but the serious guys go with crab or worm.

The kick-off for some fine flounder fishing starts again in November as the flatties move inshore to feed and then snooze before starting their annual ritual again the next year. This is the time to catch the biggest ones. Use Election Day, for example, as "GO!" Marty likes to see the flags at rest, meaning light wind, and have a moving tide. This ideal set of conditions will cause him to drift the Staten Island side and, yes, DRIFT FOR FLOUNDER. Sandworm works well but a properly presented strip of skimmer clam tongue is usually a lot better.

In South Amboy, I visited with Kash at Fred's B&T. The large store is located at 2001 Highway 35. Another well equipped outfit that is right on Raritan Bay is Keyport Marine Basin at 340 W. Front Street. This store can not only sell you all the bait & tackle you want, they are a full service marina too. Bob told me that he does not fish much but knows that his stomping grounds are quite good. Next stop was at Pedersen Marine and I climbed a ladder to talk with Gary Pedersen who was up to his elbows in repairs to a beautiful older boat. Gary is also the Commodore of the Keyport Yacht Club and he put me in touch with a fellow who works part time at the club, Walter Neumann, known in Western New Jersey as "Walleye Wally." Wally lives right on Raritan Bay and it is his favorite honey hole.

Here is what these fellows told me.

April through June finds flounder early in April starting under the Morgan Bridge where outgoing tides produce flatties on sand and bloodworm with chumming a must. The red side of Reach Channel is a good area. Buoys 14 & 20 are hot spots, even for headboats. Joe Julian of Julian's feels that Flynn's Knoll is where to find better flounder activity on incoming tides.

Walleye Wally said that striped bass appear in the bay early in April, sometimes even late March, right after they leave the Hudson and guys fishing from shore really do well casting from

Morgan, Cliffwood, Pebble (Union) and Port Monmouth beaches. Go with blood, tape or sandworms on sliding pyramid sinker rigs with a three foot leader. Hang onto the rod because a cow could drag it into the drink in a heartbeat otherwise. When the day is dark or the water is murky, stripers can be taken at any time of the day within two hours of high tide, before or after. On bright, clear water days, this tide produces action best very early or late in the day only.

Kash said schoolie stripers appear later in April under the Victory Bridge where sandworms produce just off bottom. Also small Rebel or Rat-L-Spot plugs in white body with blue or black back. Phil Sciortino Jr. of the Tackle Box said that the Spy House at Port Monmouth has a nice showing of bass too in April. These are usually schoolies.

According to Wally, Cliffwood Beach is a spot to find bluefish late in April on metal.

May finds winter flounder in modest number but usually in large size in open waters of the Tottenville section of Staten Island in front of the Catamaran.

Cocktail blues show up at Buoy 1 in Keyport in May by the thousands! 007 Ava style jigs are tops. Just look for birds and prepare for wild action.

Early arriving fluke appear in shallow spots near the beaches but remember when a fluke is a throwback and later becomes a keeper, O-k? 5-6 feet of water is all you need early with squid and spearing, sand eel or killy the bait.

Blackfish can be found in May too at Buoys 20 and 42 at the rock piles. The Old Orchard Light House and West Bank lights are good. Also the wreck at the 17 buoy. Slack tides are best with sand or clam early and then fiddler crab.

Fluke fishing improves in June and the Reach Channel in deeper water is better. Princess Bay in Staten Island, between Great Kills and Tottenville is a fine area for summer flatfish. Some winter flounder remain too but those with teeth are the prime goal at buoy 19, Great Kills, and the Twin Islands (Hoffman & Swinburne). Early season fluke prefer outgoing tide, Kash said.

A customer of Fred's B&T holding a late summer '94 bass.

Hot fishing for fluke is often found between July and September with incoming tides best. Deeper water is better and styles are the same. Simple is best with sinker small enough to hold bottom and drift. "White bait" — squid strip or fluke flutter belly and then a killy. Just remember that the flutter belly use requires you to have the rest of the intact fluke on hand or else someone might write you up. Now doesn't that just take the cake?

Stripers are in the bay all summer and not fished for much. Drifting worms or live eels in the back of the bay are best. Another way to find bass in the summer is with subdued color jig teasers in wine, lavender or black.

Umbrella rigs trolled between Keyport and Great Kills early in the morning are a way to find blues and bass in the summer. Larger blues can be taken with clean metal jigs as well as ones with fluorescent tubes in hot pink, red or yellow.

Weakfish appear mid-July with August the best time. Fishing Reach Channel drop-offs with sandworm and small float to lift the bait up above the fluke who think they like wigglers is a smart move. The channel is as shallow as 18 feet on the other side, and then Wally said there is a 30 foot ledge, dropping to 45 feet in the

Walter Neumann holding slammer bluefish that hit a live peanut bunker, 10/94.

deep. If you can find that 30 foot ledge and drift back and forth over it, you are on Ground Zero for sea trout. Try between buoys 6 and 12.

As October appears, blackfishing gets better again in the same spots we spoke about earlier. Also try buoy 44 and at the Staten Island Monastery. Fall 'tog want green crab or fiddlers.

Bluefish the size of logs, up to 20 pounds, go for small peanut sized live bunker that can be snagged and used for bait on light wired hooks. Neumann goes with light tackle and sometimes a blue will keep him busy for many, many minutes!

Striped bass are good in the autumn at dark on plugs, as well as with live eels, bunker or herring. In fact, blues and stripers will remain until the water temperature drops below 50 degrees. Chunk bunker from shore too.

The biggest, fattest, best tasting and strongest fighting flounder come back in the fall, and not many people fish for them! Try where we spoke about in the spring, along with the main channel at Crab Island off of South River. Ditto Morgan Creek at the Parkway Bridge. The red side of the Reach Channel on the Staten Island side at buoys 14, 16 and 18 in deep water is great with bloodworm.

I spent some time talking too to Joe Lauro who works at Ray's Sport Shop on Route 22, North Plainfield, where you can buy all kinds of sporting goods, and hit a firing range as well. Joe loves to fish Raritan Bay, starting way back in the outfall of the Raritan River itself early in April for stripers. He likes to throw white or silver/white Luhr Jensen Crippled Herring lures in either 1½ or 3 ounce, as well as large Rooster Tails and Hopkins. He fishes the southerly shore and thinks that "West is Best."

Joe also likes to fish for weakfish in Raritan Bay and his dad, Joe Sr., used to say "When the azalea's abound, the weakfish are around," so use that as a good rule of thumb.

Boat Rentals

The only place that I could find in Raritan Bay is the Heavy Metal Marina under the Morgan Bridge. Sorry, but while others may exist, I could not locate any.

Boat Ramps

Here we have plenty, and for strong guys with good vehicles and small boats, you have a zillion hunks of sand to drag the rig down to also. The Heavy Metal Marina has a ramp in addition to its rental boats. In Keyport, at the end of the Municipal Fishing Pier, is another fee ramp. A good ramp is at the South Amboy Boat Club which is free to town residents. Sayreville has a ramp and in Seawarren on Route 35, Keasby, we have another.

Shore Fishing

As noted, this hunk of water offers casting rights to many locations and folks who want to avoid a bouncing boat and still have a shot at fine action can wander all up and down the bay and chuck out for fun fishing. Best known, no doubt, is the Keansburg

Pier. It is located at the end of Main Street in town. You pay a fee per pole and fishermen find flounder, fluke, crabs and porgies here, even some blues and weakfish. The Keyport Pier requires a fee to be paid and it is right at the Yee Cottage Inn. Remember that a ramp is here too. Phil Sciortino Jr. of the Tackle Box said that the Keyport Dock is "On Fire" sometimes with bluefish!

Lawrence Harbor has a jetty that will be good for blues on metal in May. At Pebble Beach, the last two hours of tide in and first two out are best.

Remember that guys who fish the beaches themselves do super for bass in the spring on worms. South Amboy, Morgan, Cliffwood, Laurence Harbor, all do it. You can also fish from under the bridge at South Amboy.

The Beach at the Spy House Museum at Port Monmouth is good early or late in the day for stripers.

Maybe the best place for grownups and kids alike is the pier that was built by Perth Amboy to act as a "wave screen," to protect the marina, and at the same time, provide recreation for fishing enthusiasts.

Marty Haines of the headboat, Sea Pigeon, told me about this place and no wonder, it is located right where he docks his boat!

Take Front Street right to the pier, and you will see a fine spot to stand at, complete with deck and railing. The pier goes out 100 feet or so, and then forms a 300 foot "L" to protect the marina. Water depth is 15-18 feet straight down on high tide and a short cast out, it drops off to 30-35 feet.

Winter flounder are taken here in normal cold times but the pier is better known for summer flounder, "fluke," and at this time, some guys really enjoy themselves. They walk the "L," casting and retrieving, and often are stopped by a nice flattie. Top fluke of 1994 was 4 pounds or so.

The pier can accommodate up to 100 fishermen if they are kind to each other, and do not take up too much space. It produces nice sand porgy and snapper catches in late summer. Crabs are also lifted over in traps baited with bunker.

Opened in 1987, the south east corner has broken bottom in

front and blackfish addicts take some nice 'tog here too late in August and into September on crab baits.

Small live bunker often pass through and are snagged to use for bluefish in June. Striped bass are often caught at night from this location, generally smaller ones.

CHAPTER 8

Sandy Hook Bay

That super spot that we have spoken about in greater detail, the Earle Ammunition Pier, marks the change in name of the same hunk of water, here on the right side of the pier, we call it Sandy Hook Bay. Of course there is no actual "line."

My "experts" here were Phil Sciortino Jr. of the Tackle Box on Route 36, Hazlett and Joe Julian of Julian's, down the road further to the south. I missed Keith ("Duke") between those stores at Dukes, formerly known as "Manny (nice name) and Mary's." This is another well supplied store. I also stopped and spoke to Jim Molnar of the Skipper's Shop, 35 First Avenue in Atlantic Highlands. No one was at the Atlantic Highlands B&T right at the Municipal Harbor Marina but in season, this is a place to find out where to, how to, etc.

While at the marina I spent a few frozen minutes with Captain Hal Hagaman of the headboat Sea Tiger. As with the Sea Pigeon, this boat is usually in the ocean, but Hal will often put his fares into super flatfish action in the bay. Some of his favorite bay spots are "The Monument," a rock at Plumb Island, probably a former gun mount, where he fishes flounder late in April. East of buoy 2 is real good in the spring on high slack tide.

Fluke fishing begins at the drop-off of the Bug Light ledge. Between there and the Coast Guard Dock is super but holding the channel edge on your drift is important. Go with squid and killy on all tides.

Let's go through the months of the year in the Bay, starting with those three that most people would rather forget than remember, January through March.

The Bay itself is really far too cold for nearly anything but in a mild winter, we will find some flounder moving around at the tail end of March. Here, as with Raritan Bay, maybe it is better to be very rich and take a long vacation instead!

April through June is an altogether different thing. Just inside the Bay at Buoy 1 you can find ling where the water goes as deep as 66 feet. Skimmer clam, herring or mackerel strips all work for these nasty to hold but great to eat red hake.

In April, flounder leave the rivers in big numbers and also climb out of their wintering over holes in the bay to start to eat. The Pump House near the Leonardo Flats is a good place to find them. Also Spermacetti Cove at either slack tide, low or high, but Jim Molnar prefers high. In order, most prefer sand, blood or clam baits but honestly, I put the bleeders last myself. Check out the bait chapter for more details. As with all spring flounder, you really do need to chum. As Hal Hagaman told us, Plum Island at the mouth of both the Shrewsbury River is a fine flounder area. The Oil Dock, between the Navy pier and the Atlantic Highlands Marina, and for landmarks, look for oil tanks on shore, is dynamite for some huge flounder for a week or two late in April.

Striped bass arrive in Sandy Hook Bay in April. In fact, Joe Julian said that you can count on them showing up with open mouth's as soon as the Magnolia trees blossom, mid-April yearly.

There are some fluke that appear at the end of April but please throw them back, they could ALL be out of season.

By mid-May or earlier, marauding schools of bluefish will appear and if you see diving birds, get to that area with haste, slow down and throw metal. Make sure your drags work well though because these skinny blues can pop your line in a heartbeat. An Ava-type A-27 jig without teaser is often best in front of the Navy pier. The waters warm fastest close to shore so do not just stay out deeper, go way into the beach too. They are taken right off the beach between Leonardo Marina and the Oil Dock. Sometimes these blues will even show up late April, by the way.

Memorial Day in May is when you can generally count on

Jim Molnar of Skipper Shop with 4 pound fluke and 3 pound blue caught at Officer's Row, 5/90.

drifting the Bay for fluke and catching some too. Here again, as with Raritan Bay, look for shallower water and warm sun. Try and find drop-offs and fish the shallower side.

June is really, as the song goes, "Busting out all over!" Fluke in big numbers and good size begin to get very serious. Across the bay at Officer's Row, some super fluking can be done. Ditto the Pound Nets that can be seen from Sandy Hook looking west.

Big striped bass are caught in June while trolling spoons, umbrella rigs and plugs. Plugs at night, rigs and spoons by day. Out near the end of the bay at the rips, action can be wild for bass but this is nowhere for little boats to play so unless you have a bigger rig and excellent boat handling ability, do not try this area!

July begins with top fluke catches being made off the Pound Nets and again at Officer's Row. The nets butt up to a steep hill in the water where depth changes from 13 to 22 feet and they hide on the edges to pounce on passing critters. These are mostly smaller flatties. Try for them with standard stuff, but also use a white three inch Mr. Twister and killy. Another variety is a Hootchie squid in white or chartreuse with killy. Some great fluke fishing is right in front of the Navy Pier on the red 2 and 4 channel. There is a steep drop as you get into the channel and just as you drop off, count on a fluke attacking. The Terminal Channel buoys, 2 & 4 red, or 1 & 3 green are fine and moving outgoing is best here. Again, fish the drop-offs!

Bluefish are in the bay all summer long and slack changes are sometimes the best times to find them. Look for birds, or as you drift for fluke, you will often get whacked and cut off, a sure-fire signal to start throwing metal.

Striper guys find bass too in the summer but they are tight lipped so do not count on me giving you any of their secrets. For one thing, none would do it. For another, if any did, someone might kill me if I said anything. Rumor has it that the bay side of Sandy Hook from Horseshoe Cove to the Bug Light is where worm dunkers and plug throwers get results. Before or after sun is the only time to do this.

There are showings of weakfish in Sandy Hook Bay each summer and here too, not too many guys are talking. I have caught several around the Navy Pier and near the Leonardo Marina. Sandworms are best but keep them off bottom. Chappel Hill Channel and Horseshoe Cove are two spots to try. Night fishing is best with light. Go with Berkeley Power Worms in sandworm finish. Some also swear by the use of a live sandworm AND a strawberry jelly worm combo.

The Bay is loaded with snapper blues all summer long, ranging from teenies in July to "Big-Mac's" (Quarter-pounders) by the end of September and early October. Little spoons produce well, but a little mackerel strip often is great while drifting for fluke. That tappety tap and torn up bait was not a sea-robin, it was a snapper.

October through December are the favorite months for Jim Molnar of the Skipper's Shop and since this guy puts 75% of his fishing time in this area, he knows of what he speaks. He has lived in the area for the past 18 years too, by the way.

A few fluke, big ones, remain and are found on outgoing tide early in October close to the ocean.

Capt. Phil Sciortino Jr. with 26 pound bass that ate a live bunker in Sandy Hook Bay.

Fall is big-time for trophy stripers while trolling bunker spoons in the bay near the Pound Nets and B light. Ditto the channel leading into the Shrewsbury. Molnar says that "Striped Bass are king" in the fall in the bay. He likes to chum and chunk the channels in Sandy Hook Harbor early in autumn and then eel or worm bait November and even into December.

Fall finds sand porgies, small seabass and smaller keeper sized weakfish on sandworm at the top of both tides at Spermacetti and Horseshoe Coves.

Look for fat and hungry flounder from October through December. It is a shame that this fishery does not get used properly. The same fish that you catch in the spring are available in the fall. They are better then too.

Boat Rentals

There are some rental boats and motors at Atlantic Highlands in the marina but they rent quickly so you really should call ahead to secure a boat. Do not expect to show up at 9 a.m. on a bright sunny Saturday in July and get a boat. The guys in the store may laugh until they bust. This is a great spot to push off from though

Jake Hoffman on right, with 28 pound bass that went for a bunker spoon in the bay.
PHOTO: COURTESY OF JULIAN'S

because you can fish Earle, the Bay itself, and even go back up the Shrewsbury. This is the only rental facility that I know exists in the bay.

Boat Ramps

Here we have two to pick from, but as in Raritan Bay, if you are strong and have a little boat, you can find some shoreline in the bay where you can park and launch your rig from the beach. Messy, but I have done it often near Leonardo. Far easier is to use one of the ramps but summer can be murder.

The state has a ramp in their marina at Leonardo. Look for the sign on Route 36 south and follow, slowly, the drunken series of turns that will take you there. A small ramp, and not a very big parking lot, but it is a fine jumping off spot. You must pay for this ramp, obviously.

Biggest by far anywhere in the whole area is the series of ramps at the Atlantic Highlands Marina itself. Busy too though so count on waiting a while sometimes. You do have a pretty good chance here though because the parking area is huge and quite a few boats can go in and out at the same time. A fee is, of course required.

Shore Fishing

Not much sand to stand on in Sandy Hook Bay, maybe at Leonardo, but right in the Atlantic Highlands Marina, a dock exists that kids and grownup alike enjoy. Mostly for snapper, but some fluke and crabs are found here too. In fact, now that I think about it, I have caught fluke right at the Leonardo Marina exitway from the little bulkhead that is there. High tide is best.

Chapter 9

Shrewsbury River

This river runs super fast! In fact I remember one particularly funny experience with a friend who docked his boat at his Condo Marina in Sea Bright. We had caught some fish when it was time to head back to the barn. We got to his dock and from then on, it was a hoot! The tide was really cranking and swirling too and we docked "by ear." The boat hit so many hunks of dock, pilings, and other boats along the trail that I was afraid we would get arrested for making too much noise!

The Shrewsbury River starts at a point just inside Sandy Hook Bay, maybe a tad south of the Atlantic Highlands Marina Harbor breakwater. Some fishing takes place here, before you get to the Highlands Bridge, but once there, people in the know catch lots of fish. The same folks who told me about Sandy Hook Bay shared some details with me as well about the Shrewsbury. Remember too that Phil Sciortino Jr. of the Tackle Box is also a charter boat Captain and his favorite fishing spot in the whole world is right at the Highlands Bridge! Sea Bright has a few tackle stores, including Giglio's at 1123 E. Ocean Boulevard but when I tried to reach them in January, they were too smart to be in the store. This is a good location for river information.

Again, by each three month period, here goes.

January through March? Slumber time for everything in January, with a flounder or two breaking the silence on a rare, balmy day. February often involves a showing of flatties though, especially at the end of the month. If you do not see snow on shore or floating ice in the river, these are indicators of an early flattie season and a top spot is called "The Quay" (pronounced KEY). I

Typical catch of flounder as are taken at "The Key."
PHOTO: COURTESY DUKE'S B&T

had a separate story in an early '95 issue of *The Fisherman* magazine specifically about this location and rather than repeating it, perhaps you can call the paper in Point Pleasant to get a copy. Simply put though, late February and into March is the place to fish for flounder at the Key. Where is it? Pass under the Highlands Bridge coming from Sandy Hook Bay and stop! Maybe the Highlands side of the river is best and clearly, the south side of the bridge. Just look for boats and you are there. If the tide is cranking, not many will be there though, 'cause the fishing stinks on a fast moving tide. "Key" fishing is wonderful on slack water, and better 'n that an hour before and an hour after. Make sure to fish the stern, or else the guys back there will embarrass you big time. Some flounder action exists down river too towards the mouth of Sandy Hook Bay. The tide is still fast here, but not as bad as at the Quay. Fishing towards the bay is better on slack too. Head back up river towards the Rumson/Sea Bright Bridge about a mile south and you will find some more flounder honey holes. The right side of the river has several good spots and if you have the time and a depth finder, take a ride on moving tide and look for the drop-offs. This is a great way to find your own spots and it does work. Of course you can try to mooch off another nearby boat but if you do, not too close, please. A favorite place for Joe Julian is Graveley's Point (on incoming tide) where the Shrewsbury and Navesink Rivers meet at buoy 32. Joe feels that wind will mess up early flounder'n but this is pretty good sheltered water so the problem is less severe in the rivers than in the bays.

There are some early season striped bass taken in the river below the Key as early as March but Phil Sciortino says they are covered with wintering over slime. Yuck! The end of April and into May is when the striped bass make their appearance and dead under the Highlands Bridge, just north of the Quay, is where many, many "Rock" are caught. Sciortino likes to fish for bass at the Rumson/Sea Bright Bridge too. Slow moving tides are best for bass, near the end of either in or outgoing, and on the swing too, just like flounder fishing. Early in the day is often best, with sandworms, as many as three or four to a hook, on a dropper rig with no cork. Bounce bottom through the channels and abutments while drifting. The old Turnstyle Bridge, north of the Highlands Bridge by a little bit, is best. They catch bass here straight into summer. The original cement turn stands up to only five feet under water and drops to 20 feet deep. Find the cement turn slab and you are in bass heaven!

Jim Molnar likes the same period of time and added that 1994 was "The year of the chunk!" Lots of bass were taken right near the bridge on anchor with bunker chunk between 5 & 6 in the morning.

Smallish bluefish come charging back up and down the

Shrewsbury in April and May but very few guys are after them. They make their presence known by tearing up the water. Listen for the sound of little baitfish screaming at the top of their gills (no, not really) — well, instead, just look for boils and swirls and them's bluefish! I prefer the slackest of water for these fish myself.

Fluke are caught in June all over the river and some really fine catches are taken while drifting in moving tides. You need a lot of lead to hold bottom while it is moving fast but you can take fluke this way. Some folks will anchor for them on slack and catch a bunch.

Blackfish can be caught dead under the Highlands Bridge, on fiddler or green crabs on slack tide. This is a hardly ever utilized style of fishing in the river.

In summer, the focus is on fluke and bluefish, but now the crab lovers get serious too. Same deal for fluke and blues, but crab traps as well as drop-lines on slow tides will give up some superb bushel filled crab results. Joe Julian feels that August is the best month of the year for blueclaws.

Weakfish appear in the summer, legal sized but not huge, generally from 15 to 20 inches. Look for them on channel edges.

The biggest kind of fluke are eating small live snapper blues from 4 to 6 inches in the Shrewsbury while drifting a moving tide in the summer. Just remember that these are big baits so you simply MUST drop back and let them eat before sticking the steel home.

As autumn appears, striped bass will get very serious about eating live bunkers or eels under both bridges. Outgoing a.m. tide is best for them. This action is often present until the end of the year.

Winter flounder come back into the Shrewsbury in the fall but like everywhere else, they are hardly fished for at all. Folks, you are missing out on the three "F's," firm flounder fillet!

Boat Rentals

There is a boat rental facility in the river at Highlands called Schupp's. There used to be another one but honestly, no one could remember if it still is in business. My apologies in advance therefore if I slighted someone, it was not intentional.

Boat Ramps

There is a small free ramp located in Long Branch at the end of Atlantic Avenue. Honestly, I could not find out any other details but it is there! This was the only ramp I could pin-point in the Shrewsbury.

Shore Fishing

Very little rental and ramp stuff here, but plenty of land to fish from, productively too. Try the bulkhead at Sea Drift Avenue and Washington Street in The Highlands, but remember that you cannot park and start before 9 a.m. AND please clean up your mess. Flounder and fluke guys like this wall and do catch fish. Slower moving, as from a boat, is the best time. There is a park in town on Bay Avenue at Long John's Restaurant where you can fish from. Again, good for flounder with worm. If you cast out, go with a single hook below the sinker and another twelve inches about it, on a six inch leader and I betcha you will catch more flounder on that ridiculous high hook. There is some early season bluefish action on Pencil Poppers downtown Sea Bright at the bulkhead at the east side of the river.

Two more spots are on the west side of the river. Go to Sandy Hook Park and stop at the first or second lot. Walk across the street to the river side and fish from the bank near Plumb Island. An east wind is best for creature comfort and you can do well here for flounder and even stay warm a little. One real hot spot is the north side of the Highlands Bridge at the old former bridge abutment site. Cast chunks or plugs very early or late in a spring day and a striped bass could make your whole day super!

CHAPTER 10

Navesink River

The smallest piece of water in this string of four, nevertheless the Navesink holds some dynamite activity during the year. Brackish up a bit, starting at the outfall of The Swimming River Reservoir, and dumping out into the confluence with the Shrewsbury, we have lots of fish and crabs to catch here, and the where and when follow. Let me first say that the bunch of helpers I had for Sandy Hook, etc., were joined by the owner of the Oceanic Marina in Rumson, Pete Pawlikowski. He was a great help to me.

I told Pete a story that I will share with you and hope that you will agree that it is an interesting one. When I first moved to New Jersey in 1964 I went to a rowboat station called Pauel's, and all by myself, headed east under the Oceanic Bridge and anchored up, catching some nice winter flounder. Getting back to shore, as I got in my old Rambler wagon, I saw a boat that yelled out, "MANNY, PLEASE" to me. not exactly loaded with dough, I talked to Mr. Pauel and negotiated a price of $60 for this used aluminum eight foot Viking rowboat, complete with two green oars, a seat cushion, and anchor. The rig was lifted and stuck into the back of the wagon and it fit like a glove, sort of.

Next week I was back to the same place and, probably illegally, put the "Karp Katcher" into the drink on the north side of the river, across from the rowboat station. Rowing out and under the bridge, I tried to anchor where I fished the week before and as I threw the anchor, came within a inch or two of tipping the teenie boat upside down. Taking half the river in with me, it was murder to bale, but that was how my career as a boater began in New

Jersey. Oh yeah, I caught 21 flounder, thanks for asking, and before selling the boat twenty years later for $75, it helped me catch a few thousand flounder, several hundred fluke and an equal number of my best friends, what I call "Mr. Man," carp!

So much for stories, now on to when and how in the Navesink.

Pete told me that the river darn near freezes solid most winters and that makes flounder leave and hold over in the Shrewsbury. There were some commercial crab diggers right in front of the marina the first two weeks in January of 1995 but that was a rare occurrence. Some flounder were also caught in January but again, do not count on this taking place often. January through February is usually dork time.

A shot at flounder will occur every March for two weeks. The fish come up into the Navesink and eat well before heading out. I fished the headboat Miss Take once well back up the Navesink and we caught some fish.

April through June finds some bluefish between 6 and 8 pounds chasing live bait. Pete told me he used to look out his window and if he saw birds diving and yelling, he was off in a shot to the dock to sling Hopkins and other metal for some super action.

Fluke appear in June and will be taken during much of the summer. Right near the bridge is great and buoy 18 is a favorite location. Look for holes and drop-off for best flattie results.

Buoy 18 is super for summer weakfish, especially on early tides with sheddar crab and doodle bug. Lift the rig and get hit as it falls. Sand worm works great.

An enemy of all people, competing with the fluke and weakies and not exactly loved by anyone, is what Pete calls "Sally-Growlers." My name for them has always been "Uggglies." Some call them Oyster Crackers but their kissin' cuzzins, anglerfish, headfish, toadfish, or monkfish, all are more head than body and love to eat anything you offer. Slack water, dead on bottom, often means your baited hook swallowed up into a bottomless stomach. Their head is so big that if you try to stick a finger down their throat to get the hook out someone will wind up calling you "Nine-finger."

August brings some great kingfishing under the Oceanic Bridge with sandworms the bait of choice.

Snappers are everywhere in the summer and so numerous, fluke fishermen often have to remove their white attractor (squid, etc.) to avoid the little choppers and fish just a live killy.

Crab activity is at its absolute peak in the summer and 1994 was the best year ever, right in front of the Marina. Traps and drop-lines both produce well. Dip-netting at the pilings on outgoing low tide often is super but here you will often get a female with eggs and they must be released.

Flounder appear in October and generally stay into December before going back into the Shrewsbury when the ice starts to build up. Slower tides and changes are best with sandworm or clam, again, CHUM too.

Boat Rentals

Well, obviously first on the list is the Oceanic Marina and I highly recommend it. You can rent a boat with or without a motor. Back up the river at Red Bank, there is a facility called Sea Land at the Railroad Bridge where you can rent a rowboat too, without kicker.

Boat Ramps

I found out about two of them that service the Navesink and that is not bad. One is at Chris' Landing in River Plaza at the west side of the Red Bank Bridge. This is a daily ramp. Best known is the yearly permit ramp behind Borough Hall in Rumson. You do need a town permit for the year though, please remember this!

Shore Fishing

The Navesink is bordered on both sides by lots of fancy houses and even fancier owners. I am not knocking them, and in fact, if I owned such a joint and someone parked at the end of my block and walked out onto the end of my dock and made a mess, hoo boy, would I ever call the cops? You betcha!

One spot to fish from is at Marine Park in Red Bank where

extended stationary docks exist and kids and grownups enjoy crabbing and snapper fishing here. Lots of room too. It is at the Riverview Medical Center. Across the river from Oceanic Marina on the North East side of the bridge is an area that is good on high tide. The folks who get there early have the best shot at finding parking. Fluke and crabs both please here. There is a four foot tide drop though so again, high tide. Details about another great location for people of all ages was provided to me by a real "Authority," Geoff Piehler, manager of the Sports Authority store on Route 18 in East Brunswick. Geoff used to live in Tinton Falls and spent many a day fishing in Fair Haven, at the end of Fair Haven Road off of a very comfortable pier. Plenty of free parking nearby too, he added. Winter flounder can be taken there in normal cold water times, but more dependable are the catches of snapper, fluke and blue claw crabs during the summer. The high tide brings about 14 feet of water to the pier and on low it is only 8 feet or so, so concentrate more on high for fish and low for crabs. Geoff liked to cast a killy and squid combination for fluke, slowly retrieving it along the bottom until that tell-tale "stop" occurs, and then, slam! Don't forget to bring a long handled net with you, small opening for crab or big for fluke.

CHAPTER 11

Shark River

So, why do they call it "Shark River?" You got me! For all the people that I spoke to about this place, I forget to ask any of them why it has that name. Many of the inland saltwater spots in New Jersey are visited by sharks, especially the Delaware and Barnegat, and even Sandy Hook sometimes but frankly, I never heard of a shark in the Shark River. On the other hand, maybe just a rumor of the appearance alone of one caused the naming. In truth, I apologize for those who might be interested, but this is a fishing book, not a sharking book!

In the thirty plus years that I have lived in New Jersey, without doubt, the Shark River has been my number one saltwater river to fish. If you add up the hours I have fished in all other saltwater rivers and bays combined in Jersey, they may just equal the time fished in the Shark River. Just as a guess, I think I could safely say that I have been on the river several thousand hours. Of course experts like Russ Wilson and Mic Vassallo can multiply that many times but I really can talk to you with knowledge about it.

I interviewed three experts on the river, so let me share that information with you, mixing in some of my own stuff at the same time, and ending with a tale from an inland facility.

Let's first talk about the area called Shark River Hills. My first stop was at the Shark River Hills Marina on Riverside Drive. The town is actually called Neptune here. I spoke first with Barbara Oliver and then picked the brain of Paul Oliver for quite a while. There are, by the way, a lot of Olivers in them there "HILLS."

To get to the Marina is a little tough. Use The Garden State Parkway for starts. Get off at exit 100B and move straight onto

52   GONE FISHIN' IN N.J. SALTWATER RIVERS & BAYS

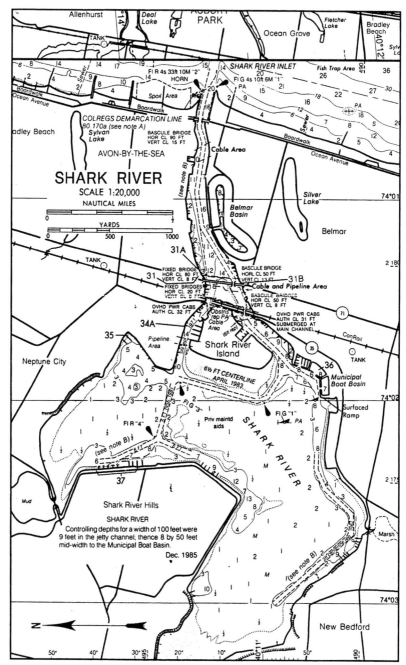

MAP COURTESY SHARK RIVER HILLS MARINA

Cousins Melissa Oliver, age 5, and Philip Oliver, age 7.

Route 33 East. Exactly 2.6 miles later you will hit a fork and a sign that leads to Route 18 North. Take the right fork to an Exxon Station and continue across the street (do NOT go to 18 North)! As you cross you will be on a little street called Route 17 and W. Sylvania Avenue. Drive 8/10 of a mile and turn right onto East End Avenue. This street will take you over the back end of the river, and as you cross the bridge, hang a left onto Riverside Drive. Head straight ahead on Riverside to the Marina. If you want to talk to anyone in the marina, just ask if they are "An Oliver." Chances are you will find one!

Paul said the first three months of the year can be real good for winter flounder. I can echo those sentiments, having fished "The Hills" at least one hundred times over winter's past. There is a six foot tide difference back in his area and even after the dredging that took place in the late 80's, 12 feet is deep so look for higher tides than lower for best fishing.

Way back, about fifteen years ago, I fished four times in a row in my little eight foot aluminum "Karp Katcher" in the Hills, taking between a half-bucket and even more than a full bucket of flatties, with hardly another boat near. Unfortunately, in that last outing, Bob Duffy, the then saltwater writer for the Star Ledger observed my luck and wrote about it early in the week. The following weekend found more than a dozen boats in my private "Honey Hole."

Anyway, back to Paul Oliver. He feels that sandworm is the way to go and only on incoming tide. The last half being best because of the depth situation. In the North Channel itself, near the marina, at the Ten buoy, he added that there is a drop off at a ridge and this is a great place to fish. You must have a depth recorder to find it, and taking the time to do so will really help.

About ten years ago I accidentally turned the Karp Katcher over one bitter cold day in February and someone called the local Rescue Squad to dry me out. I managed to scramble to safety, but without that call I just might have frozen solid. Well, I just found out while interviewing Paul that HE was the guy who made that call!

The fishing in the back begins to get a showing of fluke in June and this usually involves an anchored boat with cast and retrieve the way to go. There really is not enough area in the Hills to drift without cranking the kicker every minute and starting out again. Setting up on dropoffs on anchor with casting can give you some nice fluke results though.

Paul said that July has better fluke action, even right from his docks, and crabbing comes on strong in late August. Scoop nets around the many pier pilings near low tide works as well as traps with bunker. Small weakfish often show up in the summer, along with little striped bass.

Late summer is when zillions of snapper blues appear and little metal spoons and spinners bring great fun for grownups and kids alike. Paul really prefers early mornings for this when the water is quiet, with little boat noise or wind.

October often brings the appearance of 12 to 14 inch stripers way in the back near the bridge we talked about. He fishes night-time high tides right off the bridge, down tide, just as the tide starts to go out. A light fly rod with piece of worm on a barb-flattened hook often brings fish after fish. Best time is ten to midnight. The appearance of small finger mullet back on the other side of the bridge is what causes the bass to hightail it back there to feed.

Autumn signals the appearance of kingfish as well as blowfish sometimes. One pound or so blues also come charging back and forth. The clean water in the back of the river had a showing of small schools of squid in 1994 too, not an every season occurrence.

Even though it is kind of shallow, the best flounder fishing in November and early December in the Hills occurs just after low tide within the first few hours of incoming, as my old friend, Sam Krugler used to call it, "Half-tide." Oliver feels that at higher water the flounder move onto the nearby flats. Bloodworm and sands both produce flounder with skimmer clam another hot producer. If you could ever find sedge mussels that are legal to use, these are probably top on my list for bait and chum.

The fyke nets that had been very close to the Shark River Hills Marina have been missing for a few years and Paul and I are both very happy to see them gone. Good riddance!

If you head back out from the Marina, over the bridge, and onto East End Avenue, once you get back to W. Sylvania Avenue/Route 17, now its time to turn right. This will lead you back to Route 35 south, heading toward the Belmar Marina. Just before the Route 35 Bridge, you should see Mac's B&T on your right. This is a store that should not be missed. Small it is, but loaded from one end to the other with bait and tackle. The building used to be not much more than a little shack, actually, with a wooden counter, behind which was always a nice man named MAC, thus the name. He sold the place and it was improved by the new owners who still are there, never changing the name.

I interviewed Dan at the store and he said that the mouth of the north channel, very close to their store, often is good in January on the high part of the incoming tide. He feels that chumming is an absolute must and, in order, likes sands, bloods and clam for bait.

Bob Hall holding 4½ pound fluke he weighed in at Mac's, 7/30/94.

It gets better in the same area late in March, with February usually being deader 'n a door nail.

April will bring better flounder action in the North Channel, with small striped bass showing in deeper channels at high tide.

Flounder feed in May as they prepare to head out to sea and here the fishing is often best east of the Main Street, Highway 71 Bridge. Fluke show up in this same spot first and both varieties of flatfish can be taken in late May. Dan said the best tide is incoming with the start of outgoing good as well.

"Fluke time" is what he calls July through September, again, with incoming best to high. Standard drifting outfits produce best and if you can stand the boat traffic, drifting between the Route 71 and Ocean Avenue bridges really can produce fine results. Mid river is good, but I like fishing closer to either north or south side of this inlet area tops. Guys swear by the Coast Guard Station for fluke. It is good, but rocks can hang you up there.

As September arrives, so too do countless snapper blues, and again, just east of the Route 71 bridge, what Lou Rodia used to call "Pot-purri" occurs. You never know what kind of fish you can catch at this place on an incoming tide. I took 11 different kinds of fish in that spot one day in late September. They ranged from flounder to fluke, kingfish to porgy, snapper to jack.

Live eels are used by the real "ringers" as fall appears, around the bridges, where plugs too induce striped bass to hit. The bridge abutments often have a nice showing of blackfish too in the fall.

October brings the first and biggest arrivals of flounder at this same bridge and then as the waters cool down, into November and December, the North Channel turns on well too. Some feel that the bottom of the outgoing tide and start of incoming is best late each year.

Not exactly predictable, herring runs have appeared in the North Channel often, especially in the fall and I have had a few trips where a corn-bead hook will be hit by a herring instead of a flounder. Folks who specifically fish for herring can produce some serious catches when they are present.

We move around now, over the Route 35 bridge, and to the Belmar Marina proper. This facility is well known as a head and charter boat spot that offers just about every kind of offshore sport imaginable from fluke to tuna, but again, this book is about river and bay fishing so we will talk to you again at a later day about the available boats at the Belmar Marina.

Just south of the last headboat is the marina building itself which houses the Harbormaster, a restaurant, and what is now called "Captain Bill's Bait & Tackle." By any other name, I have walked into and out of the store many, many a day. On this particular day I talked both to Bill Brower, the owner, and to Paul Noreillie. It was January the 28th, and maybe just near freezing outside, with a strong wind cranking from the east. It was low tide and before entering the store, I walked to the town dock and saw two guys fishing! One fellow missed a fish as I talked to him, and the other guy, Dave Barreira, had a one pound flounder in his bucket that he had just caught minutes earlier on sandworm and corn bead combo. There was one rental boat to the right of us and to the left, three more boats as well. Honestly, I think all of them should have head their heads examined, but since the flounder fishing was so good in the river as '95 began, out they were. A few days earlier, in fact, Captain Mic Vassallo, inventor of the term that I stole for my Spruce Run Reservoir book, "Magic Hours," caught more than a pail full of keepers.

To get back to Paul at the marina, he said that January often remains good, on incoming tide, from just before half-tide and into just before high. Better though in March, he added. Flounder are the only action to be found. The area from the southern tip of Maclearie Park, just down the road southward on Route 35 from the marina ranging back to before the head boat dock is very good.

April brings greatly improved flattie action with the area in front of the marina itself often being particularly good. Just do not place your boat in the line of fire of some of the guys casting from the piers. After two fish, it sometimes seems like they are taking aim at you! Outgoing tide gets better in April too. Again, in front of the marina, and maybe a little to the northeast too.

Noreillie feels that May in still good for flounder on the outgoing tide during the first two weeks of the month.

June is when the fluke appear near the marina and numbers are determined by water temperatures. The warmer, the better.

Fluke get serious in July, he feels that this is the best month in the river. Killy and squid, the standard bill of fare. Paul also likes to fish a very light leader with an eight of an ounce jig, a two inch white Mr. Twister added on and then a live killy. He says this is really a great way to go but slacker water is needed with such a light lure. He likes to drift on weekdays in the exact same places he fished for flounder in colder water, in particular, at channel edges. Weekends sometimes demands anchor and casting techniques due to boat traffic.

Crab action is on in August, joined by snappers with some small butterfish. Fluke remain and the special bait for bigger fluke

Typical rental boat catch out of Capt. Bill's, 11/94.

then are the live small finger mullet that he throw-nets right near the docks.

Tinker mackerel are often caught right from the marina docks in September, and a huge run of tiny throw-back weakfish made their presence known in the late summer of '94 too, and this can only mean some super weakfishing in two years or so. Bigger weakies can be found at night in September on sandworm at high tide. A smattering of fluke are still in the river at the last of the outgoing tide.

October has a showing of flounder around the marina and in fact, Paul added, some flounder remain in the river all summer long. The south channel has had some appearances each fall of herring schools, often signaled by the appearance of diving seagulls.

The start of November is when the biggest kind of flounder are caught near the Tennis Courts and the best fishing is from Thanksgiving on. This river is far and away the most popular in New Jersey for late season flounder fishermen. Some seem to prefer bloodworm in the fall here. Bill told me he sells frozen skimmers, out of the shell, in either small bags for folks like us, or even in five pound slabs for the big boat guys. Do not go flounder fishing without some skimmer bait, as discussed in the bait chapter.

In a conversation with Will Nitschmann of Sportsmen's Center on Route 130, Bordentown, he told me about a great trip he had one day late in November of 1994 with his dad, Werner, on board the family boat, "Lottie-Da," a 20 foot Grady that mounts a 200 horse Mercury, more boat by far than is needed here, but inside was where they wanted to fish that day.

They launched at the Municipal Ramp and fished a very short distance away, right near the pier, and just out of the reach of guys slinging lead from land.

Chumming with a mixture of corn kernel and cat food in a chum pot helped bring flounder around the boat. The bait was sandworm and the hooks were model 92642 short shank Mustad beak style with bait holders, tied at the store on 15 pound leader. They fished the last part of the incoming tide, right to and past the change, and left for home with about three dozen of the finest kind of flounder. Flounder fishing continues throughout all of December here, and while there are less fishermen, there just might be more flounder too so do not give up, folks, the best may be yet to come.

I tried to break down the Shark River into three information sections and hope that this helped rather than confused you. Now that I did that by season, let's go back to the other way I have used to tell you where the rentals, ramps and shore fishing is in the river, O-k?

Boat Rentals

There are two in the Shark River, one right at the Belmar Marina we just spoke about. You can rent a boat and motor from Captain Bill's all year long most of the time, and like I said earlier, they had a few out that bitter cold day late in January!

The other facility also has nice clean boats with motors. It is called Shark River Boat Rentals and is just off Route 71 at 5th Avenue. It is situated between Havens and Hampton fish market and restaurant on one side and Ap's Marina at 610 5th Avenue on the other side. If you experience one of those very rare stinko days, of course you can stop at the fish market but try to not bring home salmon or something like that. No kitchen boss will believe that you caught such a critter in the Shark River. I have rented boats at this facility and my best summer and early fall fishing in the river is only a five minute row away from the dock!

Boat Ramps

There are three "legit" ramps in the river, but strong back and little boat guys can dunk in at many other places too. The ramp way back in the Shark River Hills is owned by the Shark River Hills Marina and you can use it by paying a fee to one of the Olivers. This ramp is small and steep but hardly ever bothered by wind.

Next is in the North Channel, and Mac's is where I go to rent a key for the day. A guard is nearly always present at this ramp to keep moochers from cheating and that is only the right thing. Two boats can come and go if they are good and this ramp is given a heavy play. You can wait an hour sometimes to get out as the late-day sailors try to launch their boats to play, making you stay in the water. This can be a mess because the tide can really cook here and cheating for position is an every day occurrence on busy weekends.

The widest ramp with the largest amount of parking is towards the south end of town, just before Maclearie Park. One in and one out can go with ease if the folks work together. Use of this ramp is controlled by the Harbormaster located in the Belmar Marina building. Here too the tide can cause some problems getting out, and it gets worse on a west wind which can bang you around pretty good, but by and large, this ramp is pretty good.

Remember that I said that a little boat is easy to launch right from shore in many spots? Back in "The Hills," I plopped the "Karp Katcher" in on high tide one day many years ago just at the Riverside Drive Bridge, catching 22 flounder with daughters, Barbara and Sue (I used to call her Susie but am no longer allowed to do so). — Susie, Susie, Susie —. The kids dumb old man got all the way down the shore that day and remembered that the rods were still in the garage! I scrounged some leader material from hither and yon and we actually took our half-bucket of fish in a few hours on drop lines!

Down past the Hills Marina is another car topper spot too.

Car toppers launch past the southern end of Maclearie Park also. Tough to find somewhere to put your car here, and impossible nearly if you have a trailer so true "car-toppers" only. Straight out from this place though is wonderful. We used to have another of those $%#fyke⅞!*nets here but it too was taken out of the river.

Shore Fishing

From time to time the towns fathers used to give grief to shore casters, especially one year when access to the prime dock, just south of the Belmar Marina, was blocked by dumping of a mountain of snow. I spoke to the mayor that year and think that this may never take place again. Folks mess themselves up and destroy things for others too by leaving litter but fortunately, enough people clean up what the slobs leave to help out.

The dock, again, at the marina, is wonderful. Read the signs to understand the rules and obey them, and you can do very well casting from shore. Folks fish from the dock at the right side, but better fishing is to the left of the marina. Fluke or flounder, nearly all the fish are flat, and slower moving water is best, especially when the seaweed is rolling in the tide. A pro can bring back a ton of weed on one cast sometimes.

Back in the Shark River Hills, Paul Oliver said that he allows people to fish his private docks and has only a few conditions. They must clean up and of course, are there strictly at their own risk. He told me about a man known as "The Harmonica Fisherman" whose daughter drops him off often daily in the winter. He walks out onto a pier and catches some flounder most days, entertaining those around also with wonderful musical renditions on his mouth organ.

Folks fish right alongside of each of the various bridges that surround the river, but frankly, this is for younger and more agile legs. They do not do as well as the falling down risk they take either, in my opinion.

The Shark River? No, maybe no sharks, but lots of great fishing and crabbing.

CHAPTER 12

Manasquan River

Most folks who go to the Manasquan approach it via the Garden State Parkway so let's use that as our way too. Our directions will be from the north, but if you are heading up the Parkway, just reverse yourselves.

Take the Parkway to the Point Pleasant exit, and carefully get onto Route 34 south. Stay on this road until you get to a circle and go half-way around it, and onto Route 35 south. In a short while you will go under an overpass and see a sign marked Brielle. I got off at that sign to start my scribbling and headed dead ahead until I reached Brielle Bait & Tackle at 800 Ashley Avenue. Lots of people helped me out with details regarding this river but we started with Greg Bogan in the store. There are several facilities located on this north side of the river, but most were shut down. A few other places for you to visit nearby are The Reel Seat on Green Avenue, and Jim's Rowboats, Bait & Tackle, on Brielle Avenue in Manasquan. Right past Jim's is Manasquan Marine Center, formerly Glimmer Glass Marina, where I met with K.C. Baney. Remember these last two places please, as we get to the Rental and Ramp sections!

Heading back to Route 35, I crossed over the river and hung a left at the light saying "Broadway," and drove east. First stop was at the charter boat, Mimi, where I spoke to Captain Dave Bramhall. Next was yet one more Bogan, Kevin Bogan, at his store on Broadway. Kevin is known as a premier rod builder, as well as a guy who knows the river. I took this road past Ken's Landing, home of the Norma K Fleet as well as several charter boats, and turned left just before the ocean and tried to find someone at what was called "Gate's B&T," but no one was at home. In season, you can count on this store being a fine facility. This path took me right to the inlet bulkhead at Point Pleasant Beach and onto Inlet Drive. A store called Alex' B&T is here, but again, not too many folks are in their stores in February! Remember this location, by the way, when we talk about shore fishing!

Following Inlet Drive around past the Coast Guard Station and back over the bridge at Ken's Landing, I got onto Channel Drive and stopped to visit with Jeff Silady at Southside Marina. Besides being helpful, Jeff also told me about the harbor seal that had been spending lots of time in his backyard.

The Manasquan is serviced by quite a few fine stores, as I have already indicated. Among them are M-V Tackle, located right on Route 35 south, just before you head south over the Route 35 Bridge. As you head south on 35, a slight veering to the right at a fork will lead you to Arnold Avenue and turning right again will bring you to Capt. Bart's. Stay in that direction and Clarks Landing Marina will appear on your right. This is the home of quite a few fine charter boats, as well as the location of over one hundred private craft, and you can even arrange for yearly rentals so when we get to the rental section of this river, I will tell you about this spot at greater length. Clarks has a fellow named Danny working there and my guess is, based on his knowledge, that he sells a lot of boats quickly, or else never sleeps because he really fishes the Manasquan area a lot! In town, and not far from a super Shore spot, the Canal, is Reel Life B&T at 2621 Bridge Avenue. Count on Rich for having up to date information and quality supplies.

Now that you know about where to get your gear and such, let's talk about the river itself and what it has to offer, based on the details I was supplied with, as well as what came out of my own memory bank. I have fished this river several hundred times, by the way.

We begin, as usual, with January, but here again, which January? If we speak in general, honestly, January stinks in the Manasquan. The water is generally too cold and the tide runs too swiftly for the wintering over flounder to even care a little bit. On the other hand though, January of '95 found loads of fine flounder fishing due to the warm conditions. In fact, as I sat down to type this section into the computer on February 2, 1995, two dopey robins were out in front of the house on my lawn. I do not know if they never left to head south or had already returned.

Greg Bogan said that the main action for flounder in January of '95 was east of the Route 70 Bridge, in front of Crystal Point Marina/Restaurant. By any other name, Kings Grant, whatever, this is a good place to fish. Outgoing tide works best here in cold water, fishing the channel edges and chumming is, as usual, a must.

The traditional kick-off for flounder fishing each year, Kevin Bogan reminded me, is mid-February but here it is strictly hit or miss depending on water temperatures. If you see lots of floating ice or the shoreline has a mountain of piled up snow, you may want to just stay at home and watch the southern guys catching what they call "Hawgs." A translator could help and do not be concerned about the way they treat their bass mouths, please.

Kevin and Greg both agree that the best early fishing for flounder that are beginning to stir after a long winter is found up on the other side of the canal at the northern end of Barnegat Bay. March is nearly always lots better than February here. As you go through the canal, you will wind up in the bay, but just to the right of this opening is the Metedeconk River too where some fine fishing is available in cold water. Danny at Clarks Landing warns that heavy rains, mixed with high tides often chases the flounder out of this section and into the Manasquan early, especially after a mild winter so do not wait long to try it. He likes to fish the south side of the Mantoloking Bridge early, and then what is called "Gunner's Ditch," just north of the bridge. Outgoing tide with sand mostly, but also with bloodworm.

One specific spot to try is just after leaving the canal going south. Head to the left and fish near and around low tide at what is called "Dale's Point." Be careful in dealing with time of tide in this area because it varies by a great deal from the Manasquan Inlet times. It could be as much as two hours or more later. Captain

Dave Bramhall takes his big boat Mimi into this same area in March, not much more than a five minute ride south from the mouth of the canal. He feels that the deeper holes must be fished in the winter near the Mantoloking/bridge. Dave feels that sun plays a big part in convincing early flatties to get serious. The rays of sun help get the flounder to start to move and feed. Go with channel edges and use worm bait. To repeat, chum, of course. When fishing this area all agree that the time immediately surrounding slack water is best. Greg thinks that a half hour before and after slack is peak.

April is when the ringers start looking for flounder in the canal itself, as the fish start to head out of the bay. You really must know when the tides are here because once you are into the second hour of either in or outgoing, it really cranks and it is nearly impossible to hold bottom. Flounder are sissies to begin with and they sure will not fight a tide to eat a piece of worm. Fish slack for best action, with sand worm bait.

Canal hot shots know that striped bass can be caught in April with slack water mandatory, and maybe a half-hour of movement too. Go with slider floats and egg sinkers, holding your sand or blood worm a foot or so off bottom. If you do not know how to rig a slider float (also called "Slip-bobber"), practice at home because I guarantee that you will screw it up otherwise as you are wildly trying to do it when fellows are fighting bass. These stripers are often between 10 and 20 pounds and must be hell to land.

Bramhall said that when the water reaches the mid-forties in April, flounder really get into eating moods, still with the slower movement best. Kevin said that the fish start way upriver in the Manasquan itself, above the Route 70 Bridge, working down to the Point Pleasant Hospital, as well as near Clarks Landing Marina and the Golf Course. Late April often has the flattie action best down river, near the Route 35 Bridge. The end of the month will find them from the 35 Bridge to the Railroad Bridge and east of the Railroad Bridge (they call it the "Train Bridge"). I call this bridge Suicide Alley due to the wild traffic it often gets. Once east of the bridge the activity is often wild on the south side of the river off of

Gull Island dead on the edge of the channel drop-off. If you do not have a depth finder this could be trouble, but trial and error and enough strength to place and haul anchor a half-dozen times will generally situate you correctly. We often see The Mimi and other big boats fishing this area before they start fishing the ocean.

May is the time that blackfish come into the river. I think it is to spawn because some that I caught were loaded with roe, but whatever brings them in, both Bogan's agree that the canal is a fine place to fish. Slack tide, again. Early 'tog prefer sand worm and clams but as the season progresses, the bait of choice is fiddler and green crab. The ocean inlet has some good blackfishing too in May with less fish but bigger ones. The canal "slipperies" are usually smaller and, please, know the size limit, folks! Guys who fish at and around the various bridges in May will catch blackfish at slow incoming water on crab bait. This requires good boat handlers only though.

Striper lovers fish in May at the bridges at night with worm, clam or live eel at first, and then switch over to plugs. Night time is best but some hit in early mornings as well.

As June appears, the main body of flounder has left but some remain, especially closer to the ocean. This is fortunate because this too is when the fluke come swimming into the river. I remember many a trip, fishing that first buoy east of my Suicide Bridge at the south side on its drop off, catching flounder and fluke at the same time on my two differently rigged rods. Greg and I agreed that a strip of fresh herring alone is dynamite for fluke early and a good thinly cut mackerel strip is also good. Go with incoming tide. Lots of early fluke action is while drifting, the traditional method, but if you can find a drop-off and the river is too filled with boats, anchor up and do some cast and retrieve fishing. Dust your strip baits from deep to shallow or vice-versa and just on the edge, whammo, often!

Clarks' Danny likes to fish for fluke in June in Gunner's Ditch as well as right in the Meteteconk River itself. He says that the only time to fish this shallow, quiet river is early in the morning before boat traffic spooks the fluke.

Jimmy "The Mustad Man" Paone with a 2 pound fluke he caught at "Jim's Drop-Off," close to Cook's Creek.
PHOTO: KEVIN BOGAN

Many striped bass were caught in the river in June of '93 and '94, starting at the Point Pleasant Canal and then to the 35 and "Train" bridges. For whatever reason, the fish near the bridges are usually small, from a foot to a foot and a half, but lots of fun. Try a lead head bucktail with rubber tail on outgoing tide near the bridges. Jeff Silady of Southside Marina likes to fish 2/3 of the way east from the 35 Bridge to the Train Bridge on the south side of the river. He anchors at night on incoming tide with live eel bait. Sometimes a yellow or black Bomber works even better. He also likes to fish right at the entrance to the creek that leads to both his and Dave Bramhall's Marina. For geography lovers, it is the second left turn IN from the ocean, and is called Will's Hole Thoroughfare. The first left in from the ocean is called Cook's Creek and this takes you to the headboats, Gambler, Dauntless, as well as to the Ken's Landing Fleet.

Jeff told me about the dredging that began in February of '95 on Gull's Island right outside of Will's Hole, as well as to the shallow water just between that inlet and Cook's Creek. Clean sand from the island was to go to replenish the Manasquan Beach sand that had eroded and the in water muck dredge spoilage was to go onto the island in place of what was removed.

July is when ocean guys get frustrated many a day. If the water is cold, with a south wind causing it, the river fills with fluke and instead of catching a zillion sea robins outside, fish the river. Just respect the fact, please, that space is at a premium. Kevin Bogan likes to fish at the old channel in front of Clarks Landing Marina on the south side of the river. Another place is west of the 35 Bridge, the first three hundred yards west of it in the channel. He likes the bottom and edges of this channel. Greg Bogan (By the way, it is true that there are more Bogan's on the Manasquan River then there are Oliver's on the Shark, but who's counting?) told me that he fished one July '94 week right near Bogan's Basin in Brielle in a car topper and caught his eight fish limit of summer flounder each day in an hour or two. He likes to drift across the channel west of the 35 Bridge with killy and squid.

Crab lovers usually start in July and here they work the pilings from small boats on low water or trap from anchored boats up river. Slack water is always best for crabs and just east and west of the Route 70 Bridge is excellent. I remember being made nuts several times in front of the former Kings Grant Marina by crabs while fishing for fluke right at the red buoys.

Weakfish begin in July with fish up to 18 inches mainly, with dark times better, and best at night itself. Very early is also fine. Fishing between the Mantoloking Bridge and the canal mouth is good at the east shore of the bay right at the channel edge. This place is where sandworm on a smaller number one or two hook works well. Ditto a jigged bucktail and rubber worm. Late July finds weakies back up the river, west of the 70 Bridge on floating Rat-L-Traps in silver and blue or silver and black. A round headed white or chartreuse bucktail with white or chartreuse three inch Mr. Twister added is super. Erratically retrieve your lure across tide, bouncing bottom. Incoming to high tide at night is best.

A few folks fish at night in July from anchored boats right near the 35 Bridge and they are catching striped bass! Use of a light will help and the style is a whole skimmer clam floated out into slow tide. Not too many people know about this and to protect his life, I will not tell you which guy spilled the beans. It does work though, often!

August? Most of the pro's feel that this is the best month for weakfish. Yes, many fluke remain but weakies are the fish of choice for steady Manasquan lovers. Go with dark times and sandworm. Jeff Silady likes to fish the entrance to Cook's Creek at night on incoming tide at the rip off of the bulkhead with sandworm at bottom. Use a two foot leader below a barrel swivel, with egg sinker letting the bait move slightly in the tide.

Danny fishes very close to the front yard of Clarks the last two weeks for fluke, working the shallower channel edges on the last two hours of incoming tide. Most of his fluke are taken on light line with a bucktail and strip bait combo. First choice on the hook is a fillet of fresh caught snapper, followed by more traditional squid or fluke belly. Also sea robin fillet, but make sure you cut away the extra flesh on the fillet and just use the reddish/white belly part, not the back. This will show the most color and flutter the best.

He also loves to fish weakies in August, back at Gunners Ditch and in the Metedeconk. The first 90 minutes of light plus just before dark is tops for weakies in numbers, but the biggest eat in dark of night. A dropping and moving tide is when to do your dark time fishing.

To get back to Lou Rodia's term for it, "Pot-Purri" time is when nearly countless varieties of fish appear in the Manasquan, as they do in the Shark River, each September. Back in the 70's we used to fish just west of the Route 70 Bridge on each end of the tide. Anchoring nearly right at the main pilings on the last of the incoming and start of outgoing was always great. If any of you ever have to appear before Superior Court Justice Graham Ross in Somerset County, try and get his attention by saying "Falling" to him. One day, quite a few years ago, I was setting anchor in the back of the boat as he was up front holding onto that same piling. The boat swung out and no matter how tall he tried to stretch, (as I giggle to myself while typing this into the computer) his last word was "FALLING," as he plopped right into the drink!

September, at that same location, plus way to the east, east of the Railroad Bridge, as many as a dozen kinds of fish can be caught. Nearly all are at or under a pound, but this is a time of the year to bring a kid with you to enjoy the superb fishing. Snappers, bar jack, seabass, sand porgies, blowfish, remaining fluke, arriving flounder, some super kingfish, and often, spot (lafayette) by the zillions, along with many other fun fish. I think that incoming really is better for this activity and again, at drop-offs. Skimmer clam bait, as well as blood and sands all work. Try some regular super market shrimp as well cut into small pieces. No, by the way, this is not too expensive either. You do not need jumbo shrimp to catch porgies and kingfish.

September, and sometimes still in August, weakfish will go wild for a live-lined spot so try this style of fishing. Many of these bigger weakfish will be found near the Mantoloking Bridge, south of the Metedeconk River and into north Barnegat Bay. Ditto at the canal mouth near the hospital and at Cook's Inlet going towards the Coast Guard Station and Ken's Landing.

Danny is still catching sea trout in September back on the other side of the canal, with artificials working best for bigger fish. He likes a ¼ ounce ball shaped bucktail in white or yellow with three inch Mr. Twister in similar colors added for flutter power. Shallow water is often best. Sandworms or grass shrimp will certainly produce weakfish, but usually smaller ones than on artificials.

Some blackfish are caught at the ocean inlet in October, and flounder own the areas closest to the inlet too. Some larger snapper blues are still in the river, along with porgies, etc., but October belongs to the largest kind of arriving winter flatfish. Look for them east of the Train Bridge and expect most to be over a pound.

Striped bass are still caught in October and into November. You do not have to only fish at night for bass, many will stay active until 9 a.m., hitting live eels along with plugs or bucktails. Kevin Bogan feels that October is the top striper month in the river and early in the month he likes to fish closest to the ocean for bass. As November arrives he tends to suggest fishing back up river more

Greg Bogan of Brielle Tackle gave us this photo of Leo Duchesne with a 4½ pound weakfish caught summer '94 on a bucktail right at Glimmer Glass Creek.

near the Railroad Bridge.

November has very good flounder action, spread deeper into the river, with these fish working way back from the inlet to Route 70. Lots of guys prefer the last half of the outgoing tide. This is best when you are not fishing right after a storm because if so, outgoing tide will bring water that is too dirty for flounder to feed in.

The most difficult-to-predict month is December. Cold years finds this river shut down, slam bang dead, but others will see lots of flounder activity continuing. Frankly, for December, I would call one of the tackle guys closest to the river since they really know what is going on. Take it to the bank too that they will tell you the truth!

Boat Rentals

There was only one traditional daily rental facility at the Manasquan as we went to print so let me tell you about it. The place is really at Glimmer Glass Creek in Manasquan and as you may recall when we spoke earlier this chapter, I told you to remember this area, next to The Manasquan Marine Center on Brielle Road. Jim's Rowboats, Bait & Tackle, has some nice sturdy boats and I have rented them quite a few times. To find it, start out at Brielle B&T for example, and turn right onto Ashley Avenue. Go a short distance to its end and then make a quick right and quick left onto Green Avenue. Take Green Avenue over a small bridge, and turn right and go over a draw bridge onto Brielle Road in Manasquan. You will see the Drawbridge Restaurant and immediately past it, Jim's. Again, a nice place. The water is very skinny here, so motor carefully to the right, then quickly hang a left and this is called (I think) Crabtown Creek. I have caught fluke anchored here in several spots, a minutes or two from the rental dock. The river itself is very, very nearby but without a motor or a big dumb moose at the oars, make sure the tide is going out when you leave the dock and coming back in when heading back to the barn. Otherwise, boy, what sore arms will result.

Remember that I said that there is only one regular daily rental place? Well, at 847 Arnold Avenue in Point Pleasant, right at Clarks Landing Marina, there is an operation called Discovery Boat Club. This is for serious guys who want to fish a lot and not have the responsibility of owning a boat. You can "join" this club by paying a very significant fee but the benefits are that large boats, for river OR ocean, can be obtained. Call Clarks for details. The club is for long term renters only, yearly for example.

Boat Ramps

Very close to Jim's Boats, actually immediately past it at 381 Brielle Road, is the marina I told you about earlier, Manasquan Marine Center. This is where a very good ramp exists, and you do not have to worry about a single bridge to be in your way to get out to sea via this place. On the other hand, I just told you about Jim's skinny water, this is just as skinny a route to the river, but a little longer too. If the guys coming into the Marina work together with the folks heading out, all will be well and it generally is. Park your car and trailer right nearby. Backing down the ramp can be tricky because the path is short and many people are nearby to laugh at you! I talked to K. C. Baney at this facility and he shared a secret with me, which I will tell you about but frankly, it is not for me to try. K. C. said that the inlet to the ocean itself has rock piles at the jetty which house lots of (he called them "bugs") lobsters on slack water. Again, not for me, because too many boats go in and out of the inlet. If you do try, make sure it is legal time, and on a not too busy weekday with a friend out of the water to yell for you, and a dive flag flying, attached to your weight belt to show where you are. For me, again, I would rather have my lobster SERVED to me!

Danny said that there is a free ramp in the canal right at the Marine Police Station on Bridge Avenue in Point Pleasant. How's that for pleasant news?

Yet one more free ramp is at Johnson Brothers Boat Yard at the end of Bay Avenue in Point Pleasant. This is at the southern end of the canal at the mouth of the north end of Barnegat Bay. Again, thanks, Danny!

Friend Don Kamienski told me about another ramp, way back up river, and Greg Bogan said that it is called Bay Island Marine, on the Bricktown side of the river, west of the Route 70 bridge, well upriver from Peterson's Restaurant.

Shore Fishing

Both sides of the river are ringed year' round with folks fishing from the Manasquan and Point Pleasant sides, right at the inlet. They even catch fish sometimes. The most popular "Shore Fishing" spot in this river is right here, but most people pull cabbage more than fish. I have often observed them as I head into or out of the inlet and on running tide, it looks like most are trying for world record seaweed catches. The solution? STOP FISHING when the tide is cranking! They really do catch flounder, fluke and blackfish here though, not just spinach.

Another good place to try is near the Point Pleasant Hospital. Park at the side streets nearby and fish from the dock right there or the small beach. Flatties are the main goal. This is called the Maxon Avenue Pier. Weakies are here on outgoing tide at dark, as well as some striped bass.

Find the fire house right at the Route 88 Bridge and here you have a fine place to fish from in the canal. Greg told me about this

*Anti Bocs enjoying a balmy day early in '95
while fishing the Manasquan Inlet at Point Pleasant Beach.*

spot. Kevin added that there is a mile of canal and if you can find a place to fish from, it is often very good. He recommends finding the Loveland Town Bridge at Bridge Avenue in Point Pleasant. No, I do not know where that is but any local gas station guy will, bet on it.

In a conversation with Jack at Efinger's, a huge sporting goods store on Union Avenue in Bound Brook, he filled me in on the canal a bit further. While he would rather fish the ocean from his boat, he said that the canal is a fine place to located stripers, for example. Fish from the western side bulkhead, on either side of the Route 88 Bridge. He also favors the mouth of the canal itself for bass. Dead in front of the hospital, on the west side, is a top place for winter flounder. On the east side, just as you turn and head into the river, fluke abound in season. A tiny bit north of this spot is where weakfish are caught early or late in the day. Jack said that the whole section between the Route 88 Bridge and the Manasquan is loaded with blackfish on its eastern side.

There is another shore fishing area near the Draw Bridge Restaurant too. A weakfish or two are taken from this little place.

Last but not least is the south side of the river at the 35 Bridge, where you can fish from a bulkhead at either the east or west sides of the bridge.

Chapter 13

Toms River

Let's back up to the Garden State Parkway now and head down the coast further, to Toms River, which heads into the main part of Barnegat Bay.

Toms River has some fine freshwater fishing way upstream, but for our purposes, let's get off the Parkway at the Route 37 exit, and head east towards the ocean and Lavalette/Seaside Park, etc.

Again, we have several fine B&T stores in this area with quite a few in Seaside Park, as well as one or two directly in the eastbound side of Route 37. I spoke to Frank Z of Betty & Nick's, at 807 W. Central Avenue in Seaside Park, where you can buy all the gear you want, as well as get some nice hot or cold food. Not far away is Dolphin B&T at 1405 W. Central.

Frank said that January and February is when lots of people who love to go ice fishing really have a fine time catching nice sized white perch. Toms River is excellent for "blue nose perch" in the winter, either through "hardwater," or open. The biggest problem, besides determining what is safe ice and what is not, is finding somewhere to park your car, because much of this area is up someone's quiet street!

Stop in at a gas station on the south side of Route 37 and ask for directions, or simply take a ride and explore. I have found a few places to access the water, and you will too. The best known spot is right at the local Golf Course, between two points of land. A large, deep drop-off exists here and unless you have a depth finder with you, try to mooch close to someone who is already catching fish, because he will be where the fish are schooled up.

From Betty & Nick's, in open water, this area is only 15-20

minutes away in a small boat, and anchoring is needed, once you locate fish. Guys actually catch perch with a fly rod, throwing a small Clouser minnow or deceiver on size 6 to 10 hooks.

I fished the river once through holes dug by a friend and clearly remember catching a mess of them on an ultra lite rig, with double hook set up, one above and the other below a half-ounce dipsey sinker. Drop it down and explore various depths unless you have a recorder that shows where they are. If you find them, there will usually be lots more around. Best bait is a small live killy but grass shrimp or pieces of bloodworm work well too. Just, please, leave those little tin cans that generally contain squashed & fermented blackberry juice at home. You need ALL your senses to deal with ice and one fall in is often all you get. Perhaps the best rule of thumb to determine ice thickness was taught to me by Delaware River Park Ranger, Dave Bank, who said that if you do not see other people on the ice, you are not sure enough that it is thick enough to go out!

Frank said that the river still has perch in open water in March and afternoon is best now, while the river is running slowly. Flounder are caught at Island Heights, and under the Pelican Island Bridge, in Barnegat Bay itself.

Fishermen after flounder in April or May will catch some, but many times, their worm baited bottom hooks will be slammed by a passing striped bass too in the 12 foot depths of Toms River.

Striped bass are more active in June here while drifting sandworms near bottom and they stay around until the water gets a little too warm for them.

Small bunker can be netted in July and the pro's use them for striped bass at dusk into nightfall with a bobber and small split shot. Sometimes better is the use of a whole live sheddar crab floated down tide with a 30 inch leader.

Fluke are not present in significant numbers in Toms River, but again, you can find them all summer at the Pelican Island Bridge nearby in Barnegat Bay. This is the last bridge east off of Route 37, by the way.

Crab lovers take quite a few at night with scoop nets, off

pilings, as well as picking off those that are free swimming. You need to be fast to get these, and a flashlight shined into their eyes to blind them couldn't hurt, if legal.

Summer brings some nice weakfish action at night at Huddy Park, which we will talk about more in a little while. Lots of eels are taken here too, as well as crabs and snapper.

August and September are when the snappers get to be a lot of fun and they are joined by lafayette ("spot") with spot preferring small pieces of worm. They are wonderful bait too, besides being fun for the kids to catch.

Snapper remain in October and white perch show up too. Try a small spoon for snapper and dunk bait for the perch.

Flounder are caught in November and December, along with the perch in the same locations already discussed. Flounder are not really present in huge numbers though.

Boat Rentals

There do not seem to be any rental facilities in Toms River itself, but you can rent one at the Good Luck Point Marina in Bayville, at the juncture of Toms River and Barnegat Bay. Not far away, several others exist too, for example, Dick's Landing off of Route 9, four miles south of the parkway, in Bayville.

Boat Ramps

A free ramp can be found at "Trilco," across the Main Street Bridge in South Toms River, at the old Toms River Bus Station.

Shore Fishing

Again, ice nuts park wherever they can and one method of exploration involves taking a right turn off of Route 37 while driving eastward, say a quarter to half-way to the first bridge east. Proceed in any path you wish until you are either near the river, or totally lost. Easiest way though is to buy some bait, food, fuel, etc., nearby and ask!

There are docks located at Pine Beach and Beachwood that can be fished off of but it is possible that they are for residents only.

Best place, by far, is the area talked about earlier, Huddy Park, where as much as a half-mile of bulkhead exists that you can fish from. To find this place, take the first right once leaving the parkway and getting onto 37, and go to the Main Street Bridge in the town of South Toms River. Now just pick your hunk of land to fish from. This place is fun for crabs, eels, snapper and spot. Weakfish are even caught here at night on sandworm or small live bunker.

Chapter 14

Forked River/ Oyster Creek

Continuing south, and getting onto Route 9, I found Walt Whalen of Forked River B&T in his store at 232 No. Main Street. Walt is close to the river itself, as well as Oyster Creek, the famous Power Plant that often produces good fishing in cold times because of its warm water discharge. We first need to take a little geography lesson to understand this place.

The Forked River has three branches, north, middle and south. The southern branch brings cold water up to the Power Plant and then the plant discharges its warm water into what is called Oyster Creek, just to the south of the south branch of the Forked River.

January through February often produces some nice flounder catches on the western side of Oyster Creek with blood or sandworm. It is best when the plant is running because this brings warm water out and gets the otherwise dormant fish active. You do need a larger sinker then too though because the water is really moving.

Better flounder action takes place in March in Barnegat Bay itself, south of buoy 34 on high tide at what is called "Whale Bone" where three small holes exist and flounder are found. Do not try low tide unless you want to have a good shot at smashing a propeller into bottom.

April and May still has flounder activity but blues and bass are caught all the way up to the mouth of Oyster Creek at night on bloodworm or sheddar crab. Metal or plugs produce too.

Fluke appear in June but not many in the Oyster Creek/Forked River area, and stay on through the summer. Walt suggests the bay itself for summer flatties.

Weakfish appear at Berkley Island in the summer at dark times, with sandworm or shrimp bait, as well as sheddar crab and bucktail. He likes to use a half ounce spear-headed white bucktail that is tipped with a small piece of sheddar crab, worked slowly across the bottom.

July and August are good for weakfish in the bay, at the Clam Reclamation Area off of Stout's Creek. He also likes the buoy at the mouth of Forked River, as well as Tices Shoal. All tides are O-k, just so there is movement, and the prime time for him is 5:00 p.m. to dark after heavy boat traffic is gone.

The summer also has striped bass action in the River, and around Mud Channel, at the entrance of Oyster Creek. Try live eels, bunker or herring, if you can get them. Crab lovers like the summer also.

Bass, weakfish and fluke still are on station in September, with good crab trapping remaining.

Weakies and fluke are on their way out in October but bass remain, and November is a time that bluefish often find their way into the bay and back up the rivers. Striped bass guys generally hit the inlet at Barnegat. Other than flounder, December is pretty slow in Forked River/Oyster Creek.

Boat Rentals

Down's Rentals is at the Bayville, Lanoka Harbor line, and to the south you will find Smitty's in Waretown.

Boat Ramps

Down's also has a small ramp but bigger boats can launch at Townsend's Marina on Lacey Road in Forked River. Another good place is Rick's Marina at Marine Plaza off of Lakeside Drive East in Forked River.

Shore Fishing

Some really super fishing is available at Berkley Island, a park which has a fishing pier, bathroom, parking, etc. Just about anyone down there can give you directions, and remember, this is a great place for weakfish in dark times.

Quite famous is Oyster Creek itself where cars can park on either side of Route 9. The west side of the trestle is a good place, as is the other side of the road too. Walt reminded me that folks who fish the west side MUST have a freshwater license, or else risk getting a ticket.

Yet one more shore spot is the bridge at Beach Boulevard in Forked River, right at the Elks Club. Fish underneath the bridge for weakfish!

CHAPTER 15

Waretown

Staying on Route 9, before getting to Route 72 and access to Long Beach Island, we reach Waretown which has several very fine tackle stores. Among them are Kapt. Krunch at Indian Plaza on Route 9, as well as Moles B&T at 403 Route 9. Mike was in at Mole's and shared some of his knowledge with me about the Waretown area, but remember, that much of this territory may also be covered in a little while as we get into the L. B. I. chapter.

Waretown is at the western shore of Barnegat Bay and in January and February, Mike said that flounder and perch are caught, with the accent more on perch. The lagoons off of Jenkins Road in Beach Haven West are good, ditto Gulf Point. He said that the Route 72 Bridge at Manahawkin is a hot perch spot. Do not try ice fishing anywhere just mentioned though because it is hardly ever safe enough to walk on! While shrimp and worm work, he favors small live killies.

Late March is when flounder are taken in the bay itself at Whalebone and Meyers Hole, with some stripers too. Bass show up in bigger numbers in April with the early arrivals occurring at sod banks in back bays via bucktails.

A favorite trick of Mike's is to slowly move his boat right up to a sod bank, plopping a live eel or herring in, and then with spool wide open, he moves back offshore and sits and waits for Mr. Bass to eat, and this way, those "rock" hanging near the sod often do just that. This style keeps his bait from being killed or thrown off on a cast, and is certainly quiet and kind of unique.

May is when he fishes for fluke in Double Creek Channel as

well as at Oyster Creek with all six hours of the incoming best at Double Creek. He likes to use a killy and squid combo, like most of us, but also enjoys bucktailing fluke. A small bullet shaped one in white or green tipped with either a strip of squid or live killy is the set up.

Smaller bluefish show up, starting in the upper bay in May, and are joined by weakfish at Gulf Point, as well as at the 42 buoy to its south. Weakies are also at Tices Shoal. The period between 5 and 9 a.m. is best, but after 6 p.m. is also good. Chum with grass shrimp on anchor and sheddar bait is tops.

The whole period of June through September is where fluke can be taken in the same areas and via the exact same method, and crab trappers get busy now too. Again, incoming tide, and trappers are joined by folks using simple handlines, a very basic method but deadly if you know how to feel for the crab, pull it gently to the boat, and get that dip net under before he knows what is going on.

Stripers appear in the fall back at the sod banks as well as at the north and south jetties out to the ocean. Live eels are best but black Bombers also do it. Ditto Smokey Joe Red Fins by Cotten Cordell. A black and silver Rebel is deadly sometimes too. Mike feels that "Striper fishing is best in the fall in Barnegat Bay!"

Bluefish are not always found in the bay in the fall, sometimes hardly ever, and at other years, in big numbers. Call one of our sources discussed here before anticipating a bout with blues in the bay. Bass, on the other hand, will stick around into November and even December and in these two months, flounder re-appear. Winter flounder get little or no respect in the Bay because by then, striper guys are out fishing the ocean beaches, and could not care less about flatties.

Boat Rentals

As discussed in our prior chapter, Smitty's in Waretown is a good livery. It is located on Clearwater Avenue. Also try Mac's Dock on Oregon Avenue in Waretown and lastly, the Waretown Fishing Station at the end of Ocean Avenue. All these places that service the Barnegat area can point you to some wonderful crab areas, a favorite sport in the bay.

Boat Ramps

Again, Smitty's can accommodate a smaller boat, and Mac's has a ramp too. Others nearby are Long Key at Pennsylvania Avenue in Waretown and on Bay Boulevard, Leamings.

Shore Fishing

There are a lot of places to fish from at the ends of lagoons and streets but to keep me from getting in trouble, let me suggest that you ask our stores for directions. Mike did say that the Waretown Fishing Station has a fine pier with a pavilion at the end and this is a nice spot to try.

Chapter 16

Long Beach Island

If you look on a map of New Jersey you will see that Barnegat Bay runs all the way down from Mantoloking, just below Bay Head, to near North Beach where its name changes to Manahawkin Bay near the Route 72 Causeway. We just finished talking about the western sections of Barnegat Bay, including the waters that flow into it. This chapter will tie in Manahawkin Bay and then hook a left up Long Beach Island into Barnegat Bay, turning around and continuing southward past 72 again and down to Little Egg Harbor, ending at Beach Haven Inlet in Holgate.

I spent one cold day in January in 1995 on Long Beach Island, driving from one end to the other and talking to as many folks as I could to obtain details for you. Some stores shown may have changed their names, moved, or even closed their doors, but for the most part, I hope you will benefit from this information.

Long Beach Island offers fishermen who like to stay "Inside" a wide variety of fishing, crabbing and clamming opportunities. It is, without doubt, one of the best locations here in the Garden State and pleasure can be found by fishermen with the widest varieties of desire. Serious guys can go out in the middle of the night and catch weakies or striped bass, or late awakeners can take the family out for a few hours of crabbing. Whatever floats your boat, Long Beach Island is a fun place to be.

Bay enjoyment can be had on the Island in many ways. There are docks and rocks where you can stand and fish or crab, many boat rental facilities, and quite a few boat ramps. Obviously the fishermen who dock their rigs at the variety of marina's that dot the island also have an easy task. This place is somewhere that gives you a broad spectrum of ways to get on the water and have a good time.

To get onto Long Beach Island, unless you are in a boat or plane, find Route 72 and head east. In the eastbound lane, on the south side of Route 72, just before you get onto the main part of the island itself, you will see Fisherman's Headquarters, located at 280 W. 9th Street in Ship Bottom. This very large store is well equipped for every kind of saltwater enthusiast and you can spend a lot of time just walking and gawking at the wide variety of stuff they have in stock.

I met with Stanley who walked me through his part of the island and let's share his thoughts now.

The first three months of the year will generally be pretty dead, at least at the start, but depending on water temperatures, you can expect winter flounder activity to start anywhere from mid-February to early March. Here, as with the rest of the state, if you see snow alongside the water's edge, that normally means the water itself is too cold. Ditto if you see floating ice. Best action comes on the outgoing tide to dead low and bait of choice is usually bloodworm. Some folks prefer skimmer clam and a combination of both is not uncommon. As everywhere in the Garden State, you really want to chum to help induce the flatties to bite. Areas that Stan recommends include the 5th Street bulkhead, fishing from it itself or from your boat. Also the Harvey Cedars and High Bar Harbor areas.

April through June are good months because boat and car traffic is not too severe. Long Beach Island becomes fierce with cars in July, but not bad at all in the spring.

Blackfish are found alongside the Causeway Bridge as well as at available bulkheads. Stan likes the western end of the Causeway Bridge on the north side. Early 'tog like bloodworm and do not be surprised if you find that many of these are big spawning females. As the spring continues these areas will also be invaded by pesky bergals and crab bait becomes your best bet.

Once the water temperature hits the mid-fifties you can count on weakfish activity to begin. Weakfish seem to be the fish of choice in this area and for good reason. There are lots of them, but the serious guys far out fish the casual folk. Stan prefers a running tide where flats are washed by the tide, fishing below the flat. Night-time sea trout lovers enjoy best results while fishing at illuminated areas. Chumming with grass shrimp is most popular and a variety of baits and lures are used to catch the fish drawn to the chum.

Some fluke can be found near the causeway late in the spring with the west side of the bay pretty good. The Middle Grounds is another place to fish for summer flatfish.

July through September brings a wide variety of fish and a huge number of tourists to try to catch them, but the ringers who go out often will still manage some super catches.

Weakfish are excellent in the summer, chumming with grass shrimp and fishing sheddar crab or other baits. Guys who jig do very well too. The White House, located at Post Island, near the Parker Islands, is one of the top weakfish places to fish in the late summer.

Taylor blues chase back and forth all summer long in this section with action being real good near the bridge on moving tide. Often the small blues will be an indication too that bigger weakfish are located just under them.

The action begins to peak on crabbing in September and guys anchoring with crab traps and bunker bait often go home with a mess of the tastiest of foods. In fact a blueclaw crab is probably among the finest tasting of morsels to me but I do have a problem with them, a big one! Every time I sit down to eat some fresh crab the area seems to be invaded with pickers. Oh, you know, a picker is a relative or friend who just wants to pick out a few pieces off your plate. A warning to crab lovers, therefore, do not, I repeat, do not ever eat blueclaw crabs in view of any other humans!

Blackfish can be found in the fall at the bridges and here the only way to go is with crab bait because otherwise bergals will kill you!

Blueclaw crabs are available into October and sometimes even later, depending on water temperatures. As it gets colder, deeper water is far better.

Action starts to slow down in the fall but some bluefish remain inside, along with the 'tog. The big reason that we do not have too much to talk about in this section is that darn near every customer at Fisherman's Headquarters is out in the ocean front, pounding the suds for striped bass. Since we are concentrating this book on fishing "Inside" only though, we can save the suds for another book one day.

O-k, we left the causeway and hit the island itself. Let's head way, way north up Barnegat Bay, to Barnegat Light and near the end itself you will find a fleet of party boats and right alongside the White Star, a place called The Marina at Barnegat Light. In that facility is a well equipped store called Barnegat Light Bait and Tackle. The address is 15th and Bayview.

I spoke with Mike Spingola and Jim Haynes, interrupted often by a loving brown creature called Mandy. Jim knows the island like the back of his hand and Mike is working hard to become an expert too.

The first three months of each year start slow but comes on strong with winter flatties. Double Creek Channel is a fairly shallow place with depths of 6-10 feet and here sunlight will improve your cold water catch. In and outgoing moving tides are both good and the top bait is bloodworm, followed by skimmer clam. Mussel and clam chum are a must. Deeper water can be found in Meyers Hole, maybe 10 to 15 feet and this too is a fine place for flounder. Same style, same baits.

April through June brings blackfish at the rock pile near the Lighthouse. Fiddlers and green crabs are tops.

Striped bass appear in the Bay late in April, along with small bluefish. Blues chase back and forth all day long but the bass prefer early or late times. The Inlet Jetty is a super place to find both. Live-lining herring in May is a wonderful way to get slammed by some big striped bass and night guys love to catch their "rock" on live eels.

Flounder remain available until late May or early June and as they head offshore, you can count on flounder with teeth, fluke,

Pete Paulaski and Jim Britton with four of their 25 winter flounder caught at Meyers Hole 3/94.

coming into the bay in good numbers. Meyers Hole is best for the switch over time and you can fish worm on one rod with fluke set-up on the other. The fluke are also found mid-May in Double Creek and then as the water warms up, they spread into the inlet channels and Oyster Creek Channel. Outgoing tide is best.

Summertime brings great crabbing to Barnegat Bay and long pole scoopers do very well at night from land with boaters having wonderful results too with bunker-baited traps.

Fluke fishing is very good in the summer with August the top month. The colder the ocean temperatures, often the better the action inshore so do not let reports of outside action being bad kill your enthusiasm. In fact, a south wind that drops offshore

*Six pound fluke caught 8/93 in front of Coast Guard Station by Frank Spingola on squid & killy.
(Or was it a "flounder" caught on a "minnie?")*

temperatures will normally mean better fishing inside. Mike likes to use a squid or fluke belly strip and killy combination, but a bounced bullet or ball head jig with bait attached is often better.

Weakies are taken in the summer on Smiling Bill jigs while chumming with grass shrimp. Of course bait works well too and chumming is a must. If safe to do, double anchoring is an ideal way to fish with a whole side of the boat being able to be worked. Jim likes a small bucktail in round head, white or yellow color, and real early or late is better to avoid boat traffic noise. Outgoing tide is usually best. If you can find live grass shrimp, they are super bait but sheddar crab as well as bloodworm work well too.

Guys who want their kids to have action without the critter being a monster find good fun with spot, sand porgies, little sea bass, snappers and blowfish in this part of the bay too, late in the summer. September will often mean big kingfish in Meyers Hole on outgoing tide. Bleeders or sheddar both work, also shrimp.

October through December means bass 'n blues come charging

inside! Live-lined bunker is super for bass and eel chuckers do well at night on the stripers. Bait and lures alike will be attacked by the bluefish that are always on the move in the bay.

Some winter flounder action starts in the fall at Meyers Hole on moving tides but even though these are the thickest, top tasting and best fighting flounder, just like most everywhere else in Jersey, flounder are all but ignored. Just think though, the ones you catch in March came into the bay in October or November and will feed like the dickens until their teenie brain says it is time to take a snooze. Why not offer them some food beforehand?

Working my way south, I found Don Tracy outside his Bay Haven Marina at Beach Haven Gardens, fixing an engine. His shop can rent you boats and slips as well as sell bait. He is super at repairs too. Don is about five or six miles north of Beach Haven Inlet.

All the way down at the southern tip of the island, at Holgate, also called Beach Haven Inlet, is Penna's Marina where I talked to Ken Jacobson who has been with Penna's for eight years. The address is 83 Tebco Terrace and is IMPOSSIBLE to find unless you see the sign on the main drag, only a few blocks before the southern tip parking lot at the inlet itself.

Ken is a serious fisherman and loves his bass! The first three months of the year are slow near Holgate, but flounder do start in March at the Middle Grounds, about two miles to the north.

April through June finds bluefish invading Beach Haven Inlet along with stripers. He likes to go for stripers with live eels.

Summer brings weakfish with shrimp bait and chum doing it early or late in the day. Try Shelter Island, just outside of Morrison's Marina in Beach Haven for super sea trout fun.

Drifting for fluke (they call them flounder as you get south of Route 72, or so it seems to me) can give up some nice catches in Little Egg Harbor. By the way, Little Egg Harbor is the name of the same water that is called Barnegat Bay to the north of the causeway. Ken likes to use minnows (again, at the magical geographical split, Route 72, a killy changes its name to minnow or "minnie," same as a fluke becomes a flounder). Ken uses what he calls a "squid teaser," cutting a strip of squid like most of us do, but then he splits the tail of the strip to create even more flutter-power! He tops the teaser off with his minnow.

As an aside, I am often asked by people to tell them the real difference between summer ("fluke") flounder and winter flounder. Forget the science folks, it confuses rather than helps to know which side of the head are how many eyes. Sure, bigger ones often are "fluke," but the perfect test is to stick your finger in their mouth. Maybe better to ask your sidekick in the boat to try this, actually. If you get cut, it was a FLUKE, 'cause summer flounder have teeth and their winter cuzzins have none at all.

As September appears, so too do the bass 'n blues and here is where Jacobson gets busy. Eel users catch some of the biggest bass around near Beach Haven Inlet.

There are many, many bait and tackle stores on "L. B. I.," as well as boat dealers and marina's. Here is only a very partial list of places to try for equipment or spots to dock your boat at.

Way at the northern end is Lighthouse Marina at Bayview and 6th in Barnegat Light. Bob Zingarelli told me that they may have some openings for slip rentals. This place houses a wide variety of party, charter and commercial boats too. In fact one of the boats located here is owned by a partner in the marina who used to charter but now goes commercial. I remember clearly a superb blackfish and weakie outing on that boat way back when I had hair, many moons ago.

Harvey Cedars Marina at 6318 Long Beach Boulevard is both a marina and tackle store. Nearby is Bruce & Pats B&T at Long Beach Boulevard and 4th Street. To the south of Route 72 is Grucella's B&T on Long Beach Boulevard and Utah Avenue. It has a super handicapped ramp for those who need one.

Again, there are quite a few other well equipped spots on the island to both house your boat and sell you gear.

Boat Rental Facilities

From north to south, in a cluster between 7th and 9th on Bayview Avenue at Barnegat Light, and not in true order for sure, are: Bobby's Boats, Ed's Boats, and Kelly's Boats. Bobby's and Ed's can both sell you gas. Next, as you get onto Route 72 Westbound, on the north side of the Causeway at Cedar Bonnet Island, is Causeway Boats.

Located to the south of 72 in Ship Bottom is Jim's Boat and Slip Rentals. They are at 26th Street and Ship Bottom Avenue. Earlier we talked about Bay Haven Marina where rentals exist too. Further south is George's Boat Rentals and Sportsman's Marina. This is in Beach Haven Gardens at Waverly Avenue and 20th Street.

Boat Ramps

L. B. I. has quite a few but parking is not too easy at all of them and of course, early birds have a better chance. The northernmost ramp I found was at 10th and Bayview in Barnegat Light. you can pay daily or buy a seasonal pass. Further south is the Municipal Surf City ramp. Look for the little town park and Surf City Marina and Boat Sales. This is at Barnegat Avenue and Division Street. (The sign said DIV and it took Stan at Fisherman's Headquarters to translate that for me). O-k, I was very cold and my brain was slightly frostbitten. There are municipal ramps at the foot of the Duck Island Bridge in Beach Haven, in the back of Shelter Harbor at 9th Street.

Shore Fishing

Perhaps the best kept secrets are these. Clearly, there are a few other places to park your car at and cast from, but tight lips exist about this subject. Obviously if someone told me and I told you about a few little spots, murder and mayhem could follow for me and my sources. I apologize therefore for skimpy details, but if you stop at any of the bigger tackle stores and spring for a few dollars worth of stuff, they might just reveal one to you. The most fished shore spot on the island is right at the very northern tip of L. B. I., and if you have ever sailed out of Barnegat, you have seen guys lining the wall and rocks up there. The truth is that fishing can be wonderful here. If space exists, park in the Barnegat Light State

Park and try your luck from the south jetty or rocks. Do not get too deep into the lower rocks though because some of those green knee busting rocks can spoil your whole day. Well do I remember a green one at Coney Island that caused me to do an Olympic style somersault.

There is a small area in Harvey Cedars where crab lovers can do their thing from shore but the exact spot was not revealed to me.

Second most well known on the island is called either 5th or 6th Street in Ship Bottom. This is a large expanse of bulkhead that gives up fine catches of flounder and fluke in season, along with weakfish and crabs. A pier may be built here within the next year. Crabs prefer the incoming tide. Fishermen find a deep cut not too far out and the north end has the deepest drop-off.

Clearly, shore casters are constantly being frustrated by the reduction of places to fish from, but this is usually caused by slobs who just do not know how to behave. Between noisy drinkers and fools who leave their mess at their feet, who can blame the town or landowner for putting up no trespassing signs? My rule of thumb for dealing with this is to size the pig up if I am watching it take place, and count heads too. If more than one guy or if taller than four feet, I shut up and wait for him to leave. Then I bag the mess. Cowardly, yes, but it works. Cotton in the ear helps cut down on the boom-box noise, I have found.

In summation, Long Beach Island is a wonderful spot for serious or casual fishermen. We have clams galore for boaters who know how and want to dig some up. Remember the rules though, and forget Sunday's! Crabbers find superb netting on the island and darn near a dozen kinds of fish are available just minutes from land. ENJOY!

Mullica River

One of the most famous bodies of water in New Jersey for two very different species of fish is the Mullica. Anyone who has ever read a single word in any saltwater column knows a little about them. Ice fishermen know that Collins Cove, located on the west side of the Parkway Bridge, on the south side of the river itself, is spectacular at times for white perch. Even in open water in the winter, perch fishermen have a ball. Yet another well known fish and location is the weakie, with the so-called "Mouth of the Mullica" being where many are caught. I spoke to Nuncie Bruno, proprietor of the Chestnut Neck Boat Yard, located just off the Parkway in Port Republic, and he was quite helpful.

Your fearless reporter has fished out of Chestnut Neck a dozen or so times, getting lost just about every time as I tried to find the series of "cuts" that lead you from Chestnut Neck to the mouth of the river. It was so bad one day that friend Tom Ross and I got so incredibly lost in an outrageously long and terrible rainstorm that I wound up expanding, harumph, the story a bit and entering it into a Liar's Contest that was held by Cortland Tackle. It was a good enough pile of fibs to win a second place finish for me in this nationwide contest, but most of the story was true. If and when you ever try to find either the throat of the Mullica, or worse, its "mouth," listen, and make them repeat directions, get two maps, seven compasses, and bring lots of extra fuel too, please. Also be certain that it is not foggy or pouring cats and dogs, because you may never be seen again otherwise.

Nuncie said that the water in Collins Cove ranges from nine to 35 feet in depth and that there is really no specific pattern followed by the perch. It is a matter of trial and error before you find them. A fish-finder with its transducer mounted on a board that you can place into the water is a great help. Bruno prefers to use a high-low crappie rig, tied with #4 hooks, which he baits with either live grass shrimp or minnows. He warns people to carry floatation onto the ice, just in case, because even in January and February, ice thickness is not always guaranteed safe.

He said that "March is the time to fish for stripers." Bring blood worm and fish out at Graveling Point at dead low and the whole incoming tide, but back closer to his docks, many head up river into Log Bay where gold with black floating Rebel plugs catch their share. Try popping plugs as well for these bass that range from 18 to 30 inches. Try ½ to ¾ of the way up to high tide, and it is best just as the water reaches the edge of the meadow.

Mother's Day in May is his official kick-off of the weakfish season, and he starts to stock sheddar crab then. Nuncie swears that this is the ONLY bait to use. He likes the slack changes, preferring low tide, and uses a high-low rig at spots like Blood Point to start, and then the Five Ditches. Smaller fish begin in May and then the larger ones appear in June and into July.

I have had some real nice catches of weakies at both the mouth and the "throat" of the Mullica. Most on sheddar, but a few too on squid strip on a top hook non-weighted bucktail.

Bluefish come in sometime in June and fluke ("flounder") are right with them. Graveling Point is where he chums with chunk bait and uses cut bait to catch his blues, as well as between the #1 and #2 light. Fluke are there also.

There is usually a wonderful run of blueclaw crabs all summer long in the Mullica, and they are most active on the last half of the outgoing tide plus the very start of incoming. Try in front of the Mosquito Ditches with handlines preferred over traps.

August and September are fine at the mouth of the river for kingfish and large sand porgies, with 1994 the best in many a year for the porgies. Bloodworm works, but he still prefers a very small piece of sheddar. Perch and snappers are around all summer as well. Some huge white perch are caught right at the bridge pilings on slack water with grass shrimp. Large popping plugs are inhaled by white perch up to nearly 2 pounds at Log Bay.

"October is the time to live eel fish for bass," he said, with many near the ocean inlet, but in his backyard, go with worms. Put a float on your bottom rig to lift the blood off bottom and away from the crabs. There are plenty of eels eating the worms too so lift a bit higher on the float to get away from the majority of the squigglers, but if you do not get ANY eels, you may be too high off bottom for bass. Nuncie fishes right in front of his place, back up to the bridge, with a strange looking rig. Spring for some bait and beg him to show you how it works, and you will catch bass!

The "Five Ditches," and "Two Ditches" are good for small stripers in November, as well as still more white perch.

Some great striper action is found up river all through December and best bait by far is bloodworm. Most of these are small so do not forget to bring a line clipper and do not try to save that ten cent hook and chance destroying the life of a possible future noble beast. Bend over and cut the line if the hook is deep. If you cannot see the hook and lift the fish to you, this could stretch its innards, draw blood, and result in slow death.

Boat Rentals
There are no rental facilities on the Mullica, I regret!

Boat Ramps
Chestnut Neck itself has two ramps, and way back up at Lower Bank, Horace Cavalier, a commercial clammer, offers another pay ramp.

Shore Fishing
Well, you already know about Collins Cove for hardwater guys, but you can also find some bank to stand and cast from nearby when the water is open. It is a tough and long walk but you can find fish that way. Use a top and bottom rig, with a fish-finder sliding float rig that Nuncie invented. BEG HIM and he will tell you how it works. You will need a surf outfit for the long casts that

may be needed for shore casting.

Before we close on the Mullica, yet one more Nuncie Bruno secret to share, involving how to use sheddar crab and not go through a zillion of them. Steal an old nasty set of leotards out of the bottom of her dresser when she is not home and cut a two inch round hole in a section. Put the rest back where you found it and no one will know what you did. If questioned, blame moths.

Insert your bait into the mesh and sew it up, or use some of that sticky wrapping thread to close. Now squeeze the whole deal and stick your hook into AND out, and go fish! The bait will stay on the hook, the squeezing will cause a modest chum slick, and weakies will eat.

CHAPTER 18

Great Bay

Look on a map of New Jersey and you will barely see that The Mullica River flows out into Great Bay. To confuse things, by the way, you may also see that, halfway in the bay on the south shore, a place called Oyster Creek exists. This may be calculated to drive you nutty because it is NOT the Oyster Creek we talked about a few chapters ago that houses the Power Plant near the Forked River. Please try to disregard this 'cause otherwise you may go to the wrong Oyster Creek and, somehow, blame me!

Great Bay eventually dumps itself into the ocean at Little Egg Inlet but along its path, some great fishing exists for those who know it. Maybe the most knowledgeable guy I know who does not own a fishing business of one type or another is Don Kamienski, and much of what this chapter deals with came directly from him. Don's various achievements include matching my tally of six "Rocket" hybrid bass one evening at Spruce Run Reservoir and participating in my best ever catch of lake trout at Round Valley, when we caught 29 in total. Our single experience at Great Bay was tooth and nail every step of the way and while he thinks he threw back one more out of season fluke than I did, I feel it was me who outnumbered him. Fortunately we each did catch three bluefish that day too, even though one of the ones that "I" landed was on "his" rod! (Hey listen, I do everything I can to not be outnumbered, and I count funny too.) This was while fishing out of Captain Mike's in Tuckerton.

Don said that you can see as many as 500 anglers fishing through the ice at Collins Cove in January and February but for me, I still think that ice is something that belongs in my drink so do not look for me to walk on water any time soon.

March is when striped bass spawn, Don feels, and leave the Mullica and head out into Great Bay. In fact we agree that there used to be so many stripers hanging dormant in the Mullica that this may be where the regulations were created that closed the season for a large part of the winter. You see, there were quite a few idiots who "fished" for these splendid beasts while using a weighted treble hook, casting either across the backs of fish they could see, or simply blindly casting out. A series of jerks and the jerk holding the rod would often snag a treble into the back or belly of a bass and this was commonplace some years back. This style of "fishing" was quite common in the Salmon River, upstate New York, but contrary to salmon, nearly all of which die after their spawning attempt, nearly all stripers do their thing and survive. That is they did until the snaggers nearly destroyed the population down in South Jersey.

The junction of Great Bay and the Mullica, at Graveling Point, is where bass show up once the water reaches the mid-forties. You can get to this spot from the town of Mystic Islands at the end of Radio Road and fishing along the bank is real good then.

Some bass move into Little Egg Inlet at the end of March and into April where bloodworm is best one hour before and an hour after high tide. Around the middle of April, sometimes near its end, is when bluefish charge into the bay and stay to mid-May. They range from the mouth of Little Egg Inlet, into Great Bay, and way back to the Mouth of the Mullica. A key location in May is Grassy Channel. Ditto the sedge banks nearby. Don likes to anchor his boat in deeper water and chum with herring chunks, as well as ground herring that he caught in the Delaware. This is the style that we fished one day in '93 and it worked. We used bottom rigs with herring chunks for bait on large, long-shanked hooks without wire. Bunker or mackerel baits work too.

Lots of blackfish can be caught in Great Bay in May at the sod banks opposite the fish factory, with crab baits. Flood tide is when they are most active there, and also at the Coast Guard Station.

Don Kamienski taking hook out of out-of-season fluke he is about to release. Note that he is alongside of the chumming board and pot line, no fool, he!

Fluke appear in May with best fishing starting on shallow flats on the northwest side of the bay. The ones that Don and I caught while bluefishing actually went for herring chunks and they were spitting up rainfish. Most go for killy and squid or bucktail with strip. Slower tide movement is best. Grassy Channel, and the flats off of the Mystic Island clam stakes are good spots. Larger fish are taken in the deeper, rough bottom near the old fish factory off Great Bay Boulevard in Tuckerton. They stay in the bay clear into late August or early September when they head out into Little Egg Inlet for a week or two before going out to sea.

Coming back to May, this is when it gets tough to pick a critter to fish for, because weakfish appear now too, usually at the tail end of the month and they stay as late as September in deeper water. The mouth of tidal creeks, including the Mullica, are early locations to look at. Tidal holes like Blood Point and Oyster Point are good. Also try Akimbo Point in the Mullica itself. Anchor in 25 foot holes at changes of tide and use sandworm or sheddar crab. The first 90 minutes of tide movement is tops and even at slack, they will feed, especially if you chum now with grass shrimp. This is also a fine time to catch "oyster crackers," slack water, and you can have every single one. Best fishing for weakfish, with proper tide, is when there is no boat traffic but you really must have a little daylight because there are too many hunks of bottom that are waiting to attack your underside in the dark.

August and September is when kingfish are caught at the slough's behind the fish factory and bloodworm is the bait. Cooler water is best for kings. Around this same time is when large weakfish re-appear and they are found at the mouths of all tidal creeks like Big & Little Sheepshead on outgoing tide. Use a white ball shaped bucktail, with rubber worm, or strip of squid and work it.

The fall brings striped bass back and, especially if schools of bait are in the Bay, small mullet or bunker, fishing anchored downtide of a tidal hole will produce often. Cast an eel uptide and let it slither its way down past the hole and hang on! Anchoring alongside of a sedge bank is another way to produce striped bass.

A run of blackfish is at the Coast Guard Station in October, as well as across from the fish factory, and calico crab that you can catch yourself in traps with bunker chum is as good as or better than green crab. Weakfish compete for the calico with the 'tog.

Don said that November is pretty slow but the inlet still holds some stripers. As for December, his advice is to GO SOUTH, way south.

Boat Rentals

You can find a nice fleet of rental boats on Great Bay Boulevard in Tuckerton at Captain Mike's. Two other facilities are also on this road, Rand's, and Mac Hoess.

Boat Ramps

Captain Mike's and Rand's have ramps and a small one is also present at Mac Hoess. Great Bay Marina at the end of Radio Road has a ramp too.

Shore Fishing

There is room for at least 20 cars at the end of Radio Road on Mystic Island, at Graveling Point. This is a good place to fish from in comfort and incoming tide in the spring will usually find striped bass present.

All the rental facilities sell bait and tackle and you can also get what you need at Scott's B&T on Radio Road in Mystic Islands, as well as John's B&T on Great Bay Boulevard in Tuckerton.

CHAPTER 19

Atlantic City Area

Known for another "hobby," this area offers some fine fishing and crabbing too, from Absecon down to Ocean City, and for details regarding this area, I spoke to three real pro's! Captain "Chollie" McLaughlin runs the charter boat, Salty Dog out to sea as often as he can, but he and his mate, Tony Christopher fish inside very many times a year too when not on a charter. Sports Editor, Mike Sheperd, of the Atlantic City Press, shared much of his knowledge with me too. Here again, most of the tackle stores were closed but fortunately, this threesome told me what you need to know. Sheperd, by the way, is no sissy fisherman, for example on February 10th of 1995 he fished a three hook rig above a sinker through the ice at Collins Cove and took home 16 nice white perch. The bait was minnie or shrimp.

There is some perch fishing going on in January and February through open water. Great Egg Harbor River, Middle River and the Tuckahoe River all have them. Grass shrimp is best with the top and change of high tide best in these 7-12 foot deep waters.

Perch continue to please in March, but out into Great Egg Harbor Bay, behind Beesley's Point at the Power Plant. Some bass show up too in March in the bays and coves.

A run of fluke takes place in April but here, make sure you know when a fluke is "legal," please. The Ship Channel between Ocean City and Somer's Point is an early stopping off spot, in shallower water first.

Striped bass lovers love April, and at Great Egg Harbor River they plug floating Rebels in five inch blue black model at high water in the evening. Fishing for them also occurs around the

Longport/Ocean City Causeway and at the Longport Rockpile. Ditto just inside the Atlantic City inlet off the rocks and here it is Bomber plugs.

Try for winter flounder in April at Rainbow Channel or Ship Channel, both behind Ocean City. Lakes Bay behind Ventnor has some too, and outgoing tide with bloodworm bait as well as chumming are all needed to produce "winter's."

Bluefish are often found in May around the back bays on all running tides once the water temperature gets over 50 degrees. Fish behind Margate at the Margate Bridge, ditto the Longport Bridge, with white round head bucktails in size ⅝ ounce. You can find them too in Absecon Bay.

A run of 'tog occurs in early May around the Sunken Barge in Lakes Bay as well as behind Longport at the Seaview Harbor Rock Pile. A sunken pleasure boat is located near Osborne Avenue in Margate and all these spots are best at tide changes with either clam or crab bait.

Better fluke fishing occurs late in May at Lakes Bay with standard minnie and squid the style. A round headed pink or white bucktail and mackerel strip often produces even better as the run first gets serious. Ship Channel is good early too, and outgoing tide is tops in May.

Some weakfish are caught in May, mostly smaller ones, on sheddar or bucktail in dark water times. The Methodist Ditch behind Margate is a favorite, and Little Panama in Brigantine too. Also at Risley Channel behind Longport.

Best fluke fishing is present in June at Lakes Bay, in fact at all of the back bays and tributaries. Small bluefish are also caught in June as well as some decent sized stripers. Go with bucktails or Rebels for bass on incoming tide alongside the bridges of Margate, Longport and Ocean City.

Fluke continue to make people happy throughout the summer with July particularly good. A top and bottom rig, shorter leader on top and longer below, drifting with minnie and squid the style.

The back bays are where some fine weakfish action occurs in July and use of a piece of sheddar crab mounted on a bucktail hook is tops. Lakes Bay Creek is a hot spot on the top of incoming tide, then through slack and into the first hour out. Tony said "You gotta' have bucktail and sheddar or forget it!"

Super crabbing is present in July and later at Scull's Bay behind Margate.

Sea trout (weakfish) are still going for bucktail and sheddar in August, but use of a six inch purple rubber worm on a white bucktail produces too. A top and bottom rig with bait on both hooks also works.

Flounder (sorry to keep using different names, but we are trying to be fair to southern people this moment who use THE WRONG NAME) remain in August, but towards the end of the month and into September, super kingfish action usually takes place, with sand porgies often present as well. Try Risley's Channel behind Margate with bloodworm or shrimp, chumming for them with frozen ground bunker in a chum pot. Go top and bottom or two hooks that drop below the sinker, and of course, anchoring is a must. The whole outgoing tide and slack low is best. Another spot is Lakes Bay where you will find a 20 foot channel but fish on the 10 foot shallow edge. Yet two more kingfish spots are at Rainbow and Ship's Channels behind Ocean City.

Fish at night for weakfish in September around the bridges with bucktail and rubber worm. Try anchoring and casting to structure and do not be surprised if the "weakfish" turns out to be a "lineside" (striper)!

Small seabass (check for size limits) join with porgies and kingfish in October, but really, it is time now for stripers!

Fish for "lineside" at night around the bridges, but to add to the confusion regarding what and where, October too is great for blackfish! Fish the 'tog behind Longport at the pilings with green crab bait, ditto at the Ocean City Bridge.

In November, the same headache is present, with blackfish and stripers competing for your attention. Use live eels by day for bass at the inlets and at night stay with lures under the bridges. The "slipperies" (blackfish) remain where they were too. Yet another fish comes in, bluefish, in the back bays in November and bucktails are best for them.

Stripers start heading back up river in December and Egg Harbor River is a fine place to try with bloodworm by day on bottom rigs. Some white perch may steal your bait here though. Night fishermen will see action on artificials.

Boat Rentals

Scott's Dock in Margate offers a variety of boats and bait, ditto Roselle's. You can also rent an outfit from Lemont's in Ocean City, as well as from Something Fishy at the Harbor House Condo's. Another well equipped facility is the Dolphin Dock in Somer's Point.

Boat Ramps

You can launch your rig at Kennedy Park in Somers Point. Also around 26th or 27th Street in Ocean City. Hackney's Boat Yard in Northfield, at the Margate Bridge Causeway is still another ramp.

Shore Fishing

There is some confusion regarding legality of fishing from the Longport/Ocean City Bridge so before you try it, read the signs! You can fish from shore around its perimeter though. There is a Public Fishing Pier on Longport Blvd., and action can be found while casting from the Longport Jetty Point. In Ocean City, the 9th Street Causeway allows fishing to occur ALONGSIDE three of its four bridges, but NOT from on top of the bridges, please.

CHAPTER 20

Sea Isle City

This chapter will take in the waters from Corson Inlet to the north, down to Townsends Inlet to the south, also including Ludlum Bay. I turned to Erich Kuehnert at Red Dog B&T for help and he sure provided plenty. His facility is at 367 43rd place in Sea Isle City. Erich not only has the store, he can rent a boat to you and for those wanting it, can also take you out to sea in his charter boat, "Red Dog," and, no, at least for now, he cannot sell you Red Dog Beer!

There are a few winter flounder taken in January and February, as well as white perch, but, even including March, his best suggestion is to spend those three months in Florida!

Fluke come into the inlets in April but again, watch the closed season time. They start in Ludlum Bay, two hours before or after both high and low tide and the channel ledge is best.

May is when fluke are both more plentiful and more likely to be legal. He likes to use a non-weighted bucktailed hook on leader below the sinker, and a shorter leadered hook above, both with squid and/or minnie. Erich said that early fluke seem to even prefer bloodworm at times.

Shortie bass are caught in May on bloodworm, again, in Ludlum Bay, as well as at the channels that break off of it on high tide, such as Flat Creek which is also great for fluke.

Some weakfish arrive in June in the back bays but only very early in the morning, ending by 8 a.m. or so. Use a white bucktail with purple worm, or a clean lead head jig with purple or bubble gum color worm. The old timers use the lead head, very slowly trolling against the tide to get the slowest possible movement through the holes and this does work!

Weakfish are in these waters all summer but as with nearly everywhere else, it is only good very early or sometimes just before dark.

"Crabbing is fabulous," Kuehnert said, from June clear through the end of the summer, at the west side of Ludlum Bay on high tide. He likes to work back into the small channels where water moves slowly and use hand lines with bunker. Traps also work, but crabbers who know how to feel for a blueclaw on a handline do even better.

There is also some fine fluke action in the summer right in Townsend's Inlet, drifting the deeper channels. Try anchoring with ground bunker in a chum pot on the bay side of Townsend's Inlet, as well as behind Avalon. Cast and retrieve a bucktail for best results on anchor.

Bluefish action is not reliable every year, but generally you can expect one to two pounders to be in the inlets in July, hitting either bucktails or even cut strip baits on top and bottom rigs.

Kingfishing has been "fabulous" in August, with bloodworm bait, using two hooks that fall below the sinker, but held slightly off bottom with a small orange or lime float. Anchoring and chumming bunker helps. All of the back channels hold kingfish at low water. Some boats take as many as 40 kings back to the dock.

The fluke activity continues in September, along with kingfish, same areas, same styles.

Try for bluefish in October at the back sides of the inlets and under the bridges at night. Townsend's Inlet Bridge is best, followed by Corson's Inlet Bridge.

As soon as finger mullet come into the back bays in October, it becomes time to go after the striped bass that are chasing them, and this continues into November when it is greatest under the bridges or at other structure just after dark. Go with live eels or black and silver Bombers. The bass are good too at daybreak.

Big blues charge in in November, and are caught in the channels behind the inlets. Ava 27 type jigs without teasers are excellent for them.

*Ernie at Red Dog B&T with strange Back-Bay catch —
3 pound triggerfish, 10/3/92*

Stripers go further back into the bay and are still active in December, but not many folks are fishing for them.

Boat Rentals

Well, of course we start with Red Dog, which has a dozen boats and motors. Another facility is Vitiello's in Sea Isle City. You can also rent a boat near Townsend's Inlet at what is called John's Pier.

Boat Ramps

There is a public ramp across from Red Dog in Sea Isle City.

Shore Fishing

The mouth of both Corson Inlet and Townsends Inlet offers plenty of parking with jetties and beaches to fish from "inside." You can also fish from the Corson Inlet Bridge.

CHAPTER 21

Avalon To Cape May

I turned to the number one authority on this area for virtually all my information, Lou Rodia. Lou has written a fishing column about Cape May County since 1952 so he sure is an expert! Owner of the magazine, *Eastern Outdoors*, and former director of the Cape May County Department of Public Affairs, Rodia really knows his back yard and was glad to share many details with me to pass on to you. Clearly, there are many well equipped tackle and bait stores throughout the county, and they will know day-to-day information quite well so make sure to visit the stores near or at where we will discuss to get current data.

The start of each year is generally the slowest inside, but a smattering of blackfish can be taken in mild times at the marina in Stone Harbor, as well as at the bulkheads in North Wildwood.

Some winter flounder are caught inside too, throughout the county, but this fishery has not been good for quite a few years so do not take a trip just for them.

The big interest in Cape May County is the offshore run of mackerel that generally starts around the end of March, continuing throughout all of April, but again, this is an "inside" book, so more on this another day.

May 1st is when weakfish move into Delaware Bay, along with drum. Back bay interest turns to fluke around the same time. Weakies show up too and a good run of seabass join in. Some are darn good sized, but honestly most are more like bassalettes. This is really the time that things get crazy in Cape May County, because you literally can get a headache trying to figure out where and what! Problems, problems, problems.

A relatively unknown May fishery (until Lou shared it with us) is the run of big blues which hit the sounds behind Avalon, Stone Harbor, and the Wildwoods. These are large fish which travel alone but occasionally they school up. The best action is in the shallow flats behind the barrier islands west of the main channels. Boat liveries offer the best opportunity to fish for these blues. Much of the flats go bare at low tide so high water is best. Use surface poppers on spinning, bait casting or fly fishing tackle. Small lead head jigs work too, as well as swimming plugs.

More confusion appears with the entry of kingfish into the mix in May at Stone Harbor Municipal Marina and at the rocks in Hereford Inlet. Take a few Excedrin to cure the headache created by the new fish that shows up, blackfish, at the rocks at the 96th Street Bridge going into Stone Harbor.

Face it, take May off and fish every day inside!

June is when fluke slow down a bit, moving back offshore, but some will still be taken all summer long. Weakfish move into the deeper holes in the back bays. Sea bass, sand porgies, spot, blowfish and small blues highlight back bay catches in the summer.

In September, back bay fishing picks up as small striped bass, spotted weakfish and bigger blues move in. Kingfish action picks up too. Some huge fluke are caught in North Wildwood in September. I remember fishing out of Dad's Place one day and getting a few, with some big snappers, but the highlight of the day was watching a woman catch a ten pound fluke 100 feet away from me. A nice run of fluke appears at the inside end of Hereford Inlet in September, as fish school to get out to sea. Lou and I fished with his friend, Joe MacGregor a bunch of year's ago at this spot and we really tonged fluke! The change of tides brought super action on both bucktails with strip or standard killy and squid. One particular moment was funny though, to think back. Two Gun Luftglass was in the back and Lou was up forward, as I had one fish on my right hand rod and the other one started to leap overboard. I grabbed the left hand rod and had two fluke on, and the boat pitched and rolled! One foot went overboard, up to my private area, and the rest of me was about to join in, but I would not let go of either rod. I doubt that Lou ever moved so fast, as he raced to the stern and grabbed hold of my shirt and dragged me back into the boat. Oh yeah, I caught both fluke to boot! My leg wound up quite wet and sore though, but not a bad price to pay for a couple of flatties.

September finds the North Wildwood bulkhead producing striped bass, weakies, kingfish and lots of blackfish. 'Tog can be caught again on the bridge at 96th street and at the bulkhead at the Municipal Harbor.

As things get colder, most fishermen head offshore for blues and stripers, but you can probably catch some fish inside too clear through the whole fall as well.

Two of the less publicized but highly important activities featured in inland waterways are crabbing and clamming. Boats for both activities can be obtained from liveries in the Inland Waterway.

Crabbing is a relatively inexpensive family-oriented back-bay sport which provides lots of action for the youngsters and an opportunity to catch a fine meal too. Equipment can be as simple as a box, ring or star trap, some bait and enough line to get the trap to the bottom from one of the piers, a bulkhead or street end, or a creek back in the meadows behind the barrier islands. As you leave the parkway and head east towards the Wildwoods, you will see lots of people doing just this! Some anglers prefer hand lines which are pieces of string to which a weight and piece of bait are attached. The weighted baits are dropped overboard and when they are pulled up slowly, crabs feeding on the bait tend to hang on to be scooped up into a net.

Some folks prefer using a version of the commercial box trap or a trot line to crab. Both require permits that are available from licensing agencies or the N.J. Division of Fish, Game and Wildlife.

There is no other license required for crabbing but other regulations do exist, and change, so be current on the law!

Clammers do need a license and N. J. residents can take them all year long. Non-residents can only do this in the summer. Lou was responsible for bringing Cape May County to the attention of a zillion people from Canada and all summer long, you will see Canadian license plates all over the road. My guess is that they too enjoy the fresh clams that are available, along with the fine fishing and crabbing.

Details regarding license, size, etc., can be obtained by calling the Division of Marine Fisheries at 1-609-292-2965.

Crabbing season generally is from early June through late October in the sounds, back bays and creeks between Avalon and Wildwood.

Boat Rentals

We start at Stone Harbor where you can rent boats for crabbing and fishing. The location is Smuggler's Cove Bait & Tackle, at 370 83rd Street.

Loads of facilities can be found in North Wildwood, and in no particular order, they are: Dad's Place at Ocean Drive, Grassy Sound, west of North Wildwood and north of North Wildwood Blvd. Then we have Grassy Sound Marina at Grassy Sound Channel and North Wildwood Blvd. Another site is Canal Side Boat Rental at 18th Street and Delaware Avenue.

Down in Wildwood, you can find Pier 47 Marina at Rio Grande Avenue, just west of Wildwood.

Boat Ramps

Up in Avalon, we have a municipal ramp that is at Bay Park Marina, between 54th & 55th Street and Bay. It is open from 4/15 to 9/15 and you can pay daily or by season.

Next going south is the municipal ramp at Stone Harbor. Located at 80th Street and Bay, again, a daily or season fee is involved, between the last week in May and Labor Day. Call 1-609-368-5102 to see if the ramp can be used without fee at other times.

North Wildwood also has a municipal ramp. It is at Fifth and New York Avenues, and as in most places, daily or season fees do apply. Another facility in North Wildwood is at Reuters Marina at 231 W. 10th Avenue. Not a true "ramp," but you can launch a boat also at Hereford Inlet Marina via a fork lift launch. This is at Ash Avenue and Beech Creek Road.

Shore Fishing

Stone Harbor offers a small free municipal fishing pier at the west end of 83rd Street. Fishing goes on there from May through November, with good crabbing in the summer. The pier is well lit and you can use it day or night. Nearby, fishing is also permitted from the 96th Street Bridge south side from a walkway. Obey the local regulations and, of course, PLEASE clean up behind you, or the clown who just left a mess behind him.

You can also use the Grassy Sound Crabbing and Fishing Pier. It is just west of North Wildwood on North Wildwood Blvd. Near that is Dad's Place at Ocean Drive, Grassy Sound, West of North Wildwood, and north of Wildwood Blvd. If that has turned you around into a circle and you are now lost, call 1-609-522-3911 for directions. This pier is available from mid-May to October.

There is a lot of room to fish from the bulkhead at North Wildwood, right at Hereford Inlet and as noted earlier, some impressive catches are made here.

Chapter 22

Villas

Well, we wrapped ourselves around the southern tip of the state at Cape May and turned up the Delaware, reaching Villas. Bayview Marina is located here, and Bob Olivio has been on station for 20 years, surely knowing the water well! His is the last Marine Railway on the eastern shore of Delaware Bay and his facility runs 750 feet out! You can find it at Oak Avenue & The Bay.

Bob does not open until May 1st, knowing that hardly anything is available in his back yard until then. Flounder with teeth (we call them "fluke" to the north, Bob) come in then, joined by bluefish, and striped bass some years as well. The start of the season is when outgoing tide is far better, bringing warmer water out. It is only a mile from his dock west to Bayshore Channel where the first drop-off goes to 21 feet at low water. This is a very popular beginning point. Bayview Marina is just about four miles from three super areas, Bug Light, The 60 Foot Slough, and The Rips offshore. We will stay "in the bay" though, since this book will keep you out of the ocean. Do not think though that the Bay is a picnic for small boaters, a little boat could flip upside down with ease in the often nasty winds that appear suddenly.

Stripers prefer live eels. The blues are found on top with artificials or caught with herring or mackerel strips or chunks. "Flounder" go for squid and "minnow" ("killy" to the north). The flounder head for the deeper edges of channels as the waters warm up.

Sometimes as early as Memorial Day, but more often, late in June, is when large weakfish sometimes show up. Not as much a

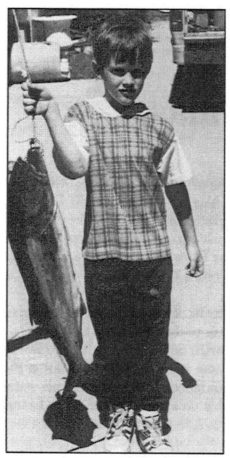

Here is a young man who fishes often with Lou Rodia. He is Christopher Hewitt holding a 10 pound bluefish caught near Villas, 6/94.

guarantee as years passed before netting tore them up, they could show up again with improvements caused by laws recently written. The fish are along Bayshore Channel early on the shore side on the last hour of incoming into the first hour of outgoing tide. Sheddar works, but Bob likes to use a squid strip, tipped with a little piece of chowder clam on a 1/0 wide gap gold hook, tied onto an 18 inch length of stiff 30 pound mono.

June, and sometimes in May, drum come into the bay and here is a sport not meant for fly-rodders or ultra-lite guys. Late in the afternoon is when this starts and into early evenings. Use whole skimmer clam for bait with a sliding sinker and fish finder set-up. A 6 to 8 ounce sinker could be needed and a stainless steel, no fooling around, 7/0 claw type hook with bait holder is the final weapon. Bob prefers a 30 inch wire leader to boot. Standard size to these fish is 50 to 75 pounds, so bring your "meat stick."

Asked "when do you fish?" his simple answer was "I never fish in a crowd," and a new or full moon is best with a hot three to four day run taking place often.

July and August is when flounder and schoolie weakfish are joined by kingfish and croaker. Try plain clam on smaller hooks with short leaders for kings and croakers. The shallow edges are good and he also likes the flats at Bayshore Channel.

Cooler evenings in September bring bluefish back, joined by stripers, and weakfish, the smaller ones, stay with flounder as well. Slack tide is best for the bluefish.

Look for birds working over schools of bunker and that is where bluefish are feeding into October. Bob shuts down around the end of October.

Boat Rentals

Well, since I asked, Bob volunteered generously that he has a dozen good sized glass boats for rent, with ten horses to push them.

Boat Ramps

No true "ramp," but Bayview Marina also has this Marine Railway, remember, going 750 feet out and he can put your boat in this way for you.

Shore Fishing

Sorry, but none nearby, this is boat fishing country.

CHAPTER 23

Maurice River

For openers, say after me: "MORRIS." Say it again: "MORRIS." Now you got it, you have pronounced Maurice the right way, just like a local.

As you head up the coast of Delaware Bay, on your way, you should see a spot called Maurice River Cove. Running up that river, into and past Heislerville, you will eventually see that the Maurice River stops in Millville at the dam to Union Lake. For detailed information on this unusual saltwater river, I turned to my good friend, Gene Zafian, who lives nearby in Vineland and often stops in at the Blackwater Sport Center to shoot the breeze with Jeff or Tim, who also fish the "Morris" a lot. Gene poked through some of the huge pile of log books that he maintains to give me accurate details, but frankly, he knows the river well enough to not have had to consult the pages at all!

The river runs about 15 miles long and has a tidal change of 5-6 feet. You will need a freshwater license at Port Creek or Manumuskin Creek, just above the Mauricetown Bridge.

Gene said that some white perch are caught in January and February on killy or grass shrimp and this river hardly ever has any safe ice to stand on. The Menantico Creek branch off the river is often fun to fish from. For example, on 1/12/95, his friends, Carl Jost and Adolph Franzoi caught five yellow perch there on killies ("minnow").

More yellow perch feed late in March and into April with grass shrimp working better at times. The Route 49 Bridge at Millville is a good spawning area for these perch. Bigger ones are generally caught in March and smaller ones the next month. They hit better on incoming tide.

Herring come up river at the end of March with, again, the Route 49 Bridge a hot spot. Herring enthusiasts fish from the bridge to the dam at Millville where a fishing platform is for fishermen to stand on, and a ladder for the fish to try and climb upstream on. Try standard gold hooks but a little green twister tail helps too. Small gold spoons also produce herring. A three hook rig with ¼ to ½ ounce dipsey sinker often winds up with a threesome landed.

As the herring run becomes real in April, count on striped bass chasing up behind them, eating along the trail. Deep running plugs are good for these bass which sometimes reach 30 inches or bigger. Try this from below the 49 Bridge to the boat ramp at Millville. Herring are snagged at the bridge on weighted treble hooks and live-lined for stripers, a sure-fire method.

The Menantico Creek gets a heavy herring run in April and part of it is quite remote. Early mornings are tops for stripers up that creek when the tide is low, using live herring. Late evenings are a good second choice, again, on low water. Some of these bass go 15-20 pounds!

The Spring Gardens section of the river is where white perch mix with small stripers and are caught on bloodworm or grass shrimp. This is about four miles downstream of the 49 Bridge. One area is called the Trailer Park, for obvious reasons.

Another favorite spot for Gene in April is a little creek behind Silverton with yellow Bomber plugs. He likes the last two hours before low tide and the start of the change while fishing from shore, although some prefer high. He gets lots of extra standing room this way.

There is a modest shad run mid-April with best action just before low tide near the 49 Bridge. Go with green herring (NOT shad) darts with green twisters for 2-5 pound shad.

The best of the striper fishing takes place in May, all the way up to the dam, and here cut fresh herring is best, sometimes just the head, with a sinker rig at bottom. Try live eels at the Silverton Boat Factory for another May spot.

Gene Zafian's buddy, Adolph Franzoi, with a nice shad he caught in the Maurice River on a green herring dart.

Come June, bass remain active, again with cut bait at the dam and at the platform. Lots of big channel catfish join in and some are as big as stripers. They eat the same bait too, to add further to the confusion.

Live eels will produce "Rock" all summer, and trolling a silver spinner with a bloodworm threaded onto a good-sized single hook is another method that I bet you never heard of until Gene revealed the style. (Well, I didn't anyway.) Low tide is still best and trolling plugs also works.

The summer has more smaller schoolies than anything but they are still fun to catch. Some crabbing is done here too, clear from May into October.

There is a good fall run of stripers further down the river, close to the Bay, and bloodworm or cut bait is best.

White perch start late in the autumn down river and work their way up. Shrimp or bloods work best for them and he likes to fish for them at Spring Gardens, maybe 5-6 miles below the Millville dam.

Boat Rentals

Sorry, but there are none up river, you need to get closer to the Bay itself and we will talk about this in our next chapter.

Boat Ramps

There is a fine large and free State Ramp at Fowser Avenue in Millville where as many as four boats can go in or out at the same time. This is about two miles below the 49 Bridge, off of Route 47. Some boats also launch at the Mauricetown Bridge on its northeast side, but this is car topper stuff only. Downriver at Dividing Creek is a gravel spot for car toppers only too, or guys with little boats and big vehicles. A few lower river ones too, see next chapter.

Shore Fishing

Gene does lots of fishing from shore on the Maurice River and again, he likes low tide because it makes access much easier with exposed land to walk on.

Some people fish from the Route 49 Bridge itself, but this gets terribly crowded when the herring run is on. Try the south side. You can cast from shore just below the bridge also. Low tide still best. People fish above the bridge, all the way up to the platform and dam.

The river is only 50 feet wide in much of its upper area but from Spring Garden down it does get a lot wider. A "cow" bass doesn't need much width though!

Chapter 24

Fortescue

There are several good tackle and bait operations located in and around Fortescue, with most of them stocking fresh sheddar crab for bait, but since I put this book together in February of '95 when nary a soul would be in their stores or stands, I turned instead to a true "Expert," and obtained just about everything you will need to know. The guy is sometimes called "The Reel Doctor," and fortunately, when I called "The Doctor" was in, it not being a Wednesday. "Dr." Ralph Knisell is a writer of fine reputation, and operates his "Reel Doctor" business out of his place at 100 W. Mantua in Wenonah.

"Not much in January or February besides snow geese or sea gulls" was pretty much the way that Ralph summed things up, but he did say that white perch are often caught in the lower Maurice River and the Cohansey River. Small minnies, grass shrimp or bloodworm all work.

Some undersized bass show up in March in the river, and April brings herring, yellow and white perch, but again, we covered the Maurice already like a blanket and the Cohansey is not too popular for any of these critters.

As an aside, Ralph said you need to have a freshwater license if you are well up the Delaware, above Fortescue, and the cut-off point is above the Commodore Barry Bridge.

Some stripers show up in the Fortescue section of Delaware Bay in April, but not many since quite a few head up the Maurice instead. Try either live eels or fresh bunker chunk for them. The end of April is when bluefish appear at lower Fortescue as well as in the Maurice River Cove. This is nearly all bait fishing on anchor. Chunk bunker or mackerel as chum and bait alike and the slow down of each tide is peak time.

The semi-official kick-off at Fortescue is May 1st when everything comes alive, the marinas, bait and tackle stores, head and charter boats, etc. This is also the time that bluefish invade in numbers to spawn, and fluke range upriver as well. Try for blues at the Southwest line to past and below buoy #1 with bait. Most are from 4-6 pounds but some monsters will also be mixed in.

The "flounder" are caught now drifting at "Flounder Alley" with squid and minnie. The Doctor prescribes a four foot leader of 20 pound test added onto his 10 pound fishing line.

Some weakfish arrive in May but Ralph feels (and most of us agree) that netting destroyed most of the bigger fish in recent years. Try for them with bucktail and purple worm, or cut bait. The better action on "tiderunners" (bigger weakies) is generally well below Fortescue.

High-humped drum show up at the end of May with full moon the best time. Ralph feels that you can catch them all day long, not just in dark times. In fact his best ever drum trip was at and around High Noon!

Some areas to fish for drum are the upper part of the Sixty Foot Slough and the "Pin Top," as well as off of Slaughter Beach, Delaware. Go from an anchored boat and use a big gob of skimmer clam on a strong and large hook. Top that off with a piece of sheddar crab "to sweeten," and wait 'em out. A fish-finder rig helps too, and the top of the incoming tide is best. Chumming with broken clam shells can help bring them around your boat. You can actually hear them drumming through the bottom of the boat in 25 feet of water, a preferred depth. This also means that lots of the noise surrounds spawning time which generally means less eating and more other things for the drum.

Drum had no size or bag limit at the time this book went to print, and they make good eating, comparing well to veal in taste.

Lots of smaller blues arrive in June throughout the bay and Flounder Alley gets a good run of flatties.

Schoolie weakfish show up in July, ranging from 1 to 3 pounds with some bigger. Make sure you know the bag and size limits, please. Set up on anchor and use a single hook with sheddar crab from a small boat. Safe weather permitting, go anywhere from ½ to 1½ miles off the beach from Ship John Light, down the coast past Fortescue to the Maurice River Cove and that whole cove is good. Some folks will go with a high-low rig with shorter leader on top and crab bait, plus a longer leader at bottom with squid strip. Go with a two foot leader below though, not four, to avoid tangles with the upper hook.

In July and August you can catch flounder/fluke (I hope I do not give you a headache with this, I just do not want to insult the South Jersey guys by constantly calling their "flounder" by their REAL NAME) in Flounder Alley, and in "Egypt," below the Maurice River Cove. Small blues are here too, from a half pound to a pound.

Spot, sand porgies, and kingfish are caught in late August and all of September, and the schoolie weakfish are getting bigger by now too. The upper bay area is best and even some 1-3 pound throw-back stripers will attack your sheddar baits. Ralph feels that the further north you get, from Fortescue to Cohansey, the more stripers you get compared to weakfish.

October is still weakfish, and some big bluefish, with fluke slowing down, and kingfish plus spot remaining. An enormous run of yearling drum appear in October as they head out to sea. Most are under a pound and disappear to parts south for quite a few years, to return once they reach 40 pounds or much more to spawn.

Fantastic fishing takes place on huge bluefish in November, and stripers too, with most guys already packed up and done for the year! Drifting eels in Flounder Alley or North East of the Maull produces some super bass catches. Inshore you can fish a mile off of False Egg Island Point and down in the Maurice River Cove from off of East Point to Bug Light and two miles south of the #1 buoy. Blues go for cut bunker chunks or whole bunker heads. Stripers eat the same stuff.

Some blues and bass are caught still in December, if warm

enough, but most people are long since done!

Boat Rentals

You can rent a boat & motor at Triangle Marina on Bay Front in Fortescue, as well as at Hook, Line & Sinker nearby.

Boat Ramps

Up at the Cohansey River, up a ways, we have the Greenwich ramp and the Hancock Harbor ramp nearby. They are both pay ramps.

Down below, we find Gandy's Beach Marine below Nantuxent Point.

At Fortescue, there is Double A Marina at the mouth of Fortescue Creek. Higbee's Marina is just over the Fortescue Bridge and this is a railway, lift operation, which can put in or take out boats at a very fast clip!

Adding to the Maurice River list, Ralph told me about the Port Norris Marina and at Bivalve, the Longreach Marina.

Shore Fishing

There is free parking at Gandy's Beach where folks fish from on high water because of the 6-7 foot tide drop.

Try the bulkhead at the South end of Fortescue where free parking is present as well.

Try the end of the road outside of Heislerville at East Point Lighthouse too.

We close with a quote from The Doctor which defies logic but some may still agree with: "A fish is the only thing that grows AFTER it dies." Well, maybe so!

Scuze me, gone fishin'

Seminar Notes:

Seminar Notes:

Personal Fishing Journal:

Personal Fishing Journal: